Items should be returned on or before the last date shown below. Items not already requested by other borrowers may be renewed in person, in writing or by telephone. To renew, please quote the number on the barcode label. To renew online a PIN is required. This can be requested at your local library.
Renew online @ www.dublincitypubliclibraries.ie
Fines charged for overdue items will include postage incurred in recovery. Damage to or loss of items will be charged to the borrower.

**Leabharlanna Poiblí Chathair Bhaile Átha Cliath
Dublin City Public Libraries**

Baile Átha Cliath
Dublin City

Rathmines Branch Tel: 4973539
Brainse Ráth Maonas Fón: 4973539

Eden Halt

An Antrim Memoir

ROSS SKELTON

THE LILLIPUT PRESS
DUBLIN

Published in 2013 by
THE LILLIPUT PRESS
62–63 Sitric Road, Arbour Hill
Dublin 7, Ireland
www.lilliputpress.ie

ISBN 978 1 84351 398 8

10 9 8 7 6 5 4 3 2 1

A CIP record for this title is available
from The British Library.

Set in 12 pt on 16 pt Bembo by Marsha Swan
Printed in Spain by GraphyCems

for Maya and Noah

Acknowledgments

Michael Bradshaw; Terence Brown; Colette Connor; Tom Cowan; Gerald Dawe; Eblana Writers; Antony Farrell; Carlo Gebler; Anne Haverty; Susan Knight; Conor Kostick; Kitty Lyddon; Seona Mac Reamoinn; Ainin Ni Bhroin; Eilís Ní Dhuibhne; Deirdre Madden; Helen Meany; George O'Brien; Helen Rock; James Ryan; Joss Skelton; Jonathan Williams; Dawn Young; Pauline Kelly; Maya Skelton.

IT WAS the last psychoanalytic session with a woman patient whom I had been seeing for some time. When she had first come to my consulting room, she had been partly paralysed and unable to walk. Now, after a long analysis, she was able-bodied and fully mobile again. As I rose to show her out, she turned and spoke: 'I must say I never really cared for you.' She paused and, as she closed the door behind her, added, 'But you certainly knew what you were doing!'

I sat down and stared idly at my bookshelves. At the top were volumes of logic and philosophy, in the middle shelf upon shelf of books on psychoanalysis, and near the bottom, at my elbow, works of literature; it looked like the layers of my life. Had I known what I was doing in all those reading phases? It seemed as if I had been sleepwalking for years, finally finding my feet as a psychoanalyst. I had studied widely diverse fields: as an undergraduate at Trinity College, Dublin,

I had felt a deep need for clarity of thought and scientific certainty. Ever since I was a boy, I had been constantly infuriated by my father's endless mysticism, speaking as he did of the Beyond as if it were a personal friend to whom only he and a few selected individuals had access. I had found a kind of intellectual home in Logical Positivism, a philosophical movement dedicated to the 'worship' of objectivity and rigorous logic – where philosophy aped the natural sciences. I had been delighted to discover that the logical positivists had referred to metaphysicians as 'misplaced poets' and religion as nonsense. Logical philosophy would have no truck with any of Father's speculations and I had embraced it enthusiastically. In retrospect, I realized that, paradoxically, I had been greatly impressed by a Hegel lecturer whose views came suspiciously close to the mystical.

At the University of London I did graduate work on logic and the foundations of mathematics for three years, after which I was offered a lectureship in logic and philosophy at Trinity. On my return to the college in 1970, to my surprise I was told I would also be teaching political philosophy. I had been for a short while at the London School of Economics during the 1968 riots – an offshoot of those in Paris. In those exciting times I had read the anarchism of Kropotkin and the early papers of Marx and, so tailoring the course to my own interests, I began teaching what I knew. My colleagues in the Philosophy Department, though dubious of my choice of teaching material, said nothing and the course became a popular one.

It was to become a strange career at Trinity, for although I loved teaching logic and philosophy, from the very beginning I had a disadvantage: I could not write. Unable to finish my doctorate in philosophy and logic at the University of London, I soon found I was incapable of writing anything at all. No articles flowed from my pen, no learned tomes emerged; however, I did love teaching anarchism and divided my time between talking with students and doing logic proofs (a form of algebra) instead.

Over the years, working in a philosophy department, I tried several times to read Heidegger and other continental philosophers, but found that my logical training had cut deep and I was unable to sustain belief in their more literary and subjective approach. In time an appreciation of continental philosophy was to come from an unexpected quarter: I went into psychoanalysis.

I had attended the Freud lectures of Richard Wollheim, Grote Professor of Mind and Logic at University College London, and I invited him to speak on the subject at Trinity. Afterwards, over a drink, I bemoaned the fact that there was no psychoanalysis in Dublin. He directed me to a small group of Freudians known as the Monkstown Group, which I immediately joined.

Discovering psychoanalysis was like coming home (almost literally because my father had read Jung) and I quickly took to it, attending seminars night and day and becoming involved in a London group studying the logic of the unconscious. My epiphany came a few years later when I was invited to lunch with the eminent Pakistani analyst, 'Prince' Masud Khan. During the long lunch, he evidently pieced together the essentials of my story and in a lull in the conversation suddenly announced, in a tone reminiscent of Freud which I will never forget: 'An academic who does not like to write?' The question hung in the air and all at once the ludicrous nature of my position was clear to me; before we parted, he directed me to a French analyst then practising in Dublin.

In the course of that analysis I began to read the poems of Louis MacNeice – a much-admired acquaintance of my father's. Before long I had managed to write and publish a few critical articles on his work. At that stage, I had embarked on part-time training as a psychoanalyst at St Vincent's Hospital in Dublin and was slowly becoming conversant with the highly subjective and intuitive aspect of that mental discipline, poised, as it is today, between the neurosciences and literature. To practise clinically I had to learn how to suspend the conscious logical method in which I had been trained and reserve it for college lecturing. The clinical course was dominated by the theory and practice of the French psychoanalyst Jacques Lacan, who had been deeply influenced by Hegel. Ironically, I had come full circle – almost like a return to the father, for Hegel, while immensely insightful in rational terms, has a mystical core, believing as he did that Absolute *Geist* or Spirit comes to know itself only by the evolution of our human life-world. As Hegel puts it: 'The owl of Minerva only spreads her wings with the falling of the dusk.' – that is, the truth of our lives can be seen only by looking back. We travel hopefully in life, encountering successes and failures, but it is only when looking back that we can see what was important. In fact, a central tenet of psychoanalysis is that whereas we live our lives forwards, we understand what Freud called our *psychical* reality in memoir.

By this time, my interest in Freud was becoming dominant and, disenchanted with the endless arguing of philosophers, I decided to start a Freud study group. But who would come? My landlady, who coincidentally was in analysis, said she would attend; so I had one participant. Then she suggested that her friend could come and when I asked if the friend was interested in Freud, she said she didn't know but the friend was unemployed and needed something to do. Reluctantly, I agreed and we began reading and discussing once a week. Before long, one or two philosophy students joined us and each week the group grew until one day the then head of department, wondering where his class had vanished to, went in search of them only to find most of his students crowding my office. The group had become so popular, he suggested I start a new course of my own called Existentialism and Psychoanalysis. This eventually gave birth to a master's in Psychoanalysis at Trinity and paved the way for a clinical course based in St James's Hospital Department of Psychiatry in Dublin.

I was still a reluctant writer and struggled on until one day I received a letter from Edinburgh University Press offering me a contract to compile an encyclopaedia of psychoanalysis. I jumped at this opportunity and put myself to work in my office – a shed at the bottom of the garden. With a view of white fantail pigeons, commuting from lawn to dovecote to roof and back, I enlisted a team of nearly four hundred scholars and analysts from around the world.

For six years I spent three hours every morning mostly on email dealing with the flood of material that had arrived from North America through the night. By lunchtime I was drained and had to rest before going to college to teach. By the sixth year I began to feel that the book was literally killing me. One morning, my then wife (also a psychoanalyst) came down to the shed and asked me to come up to the house and look at something on her computer. On the screen was an item entitled 'Burnout – signs of' and a list of six danger signs. I scanned it: I had four out of six.

With this shock I started easing back from the brink by working less. But the book was near completion – the one thousand entries, covering seven schools of psychoanalysis, were nearly ready – another six months should do it. I decided to compromise. Since finishing analysis, I had begun to keep a diary that seemed increasingly drawn back to my child-hood. It was becoming the high point of my day. I decided I would give myself the first hour of the morning to writing about where my imagination took me.

By the time the thousand-entry encyclopaedia was ready for publication, it had become clear that work on the book had damaged my marriage, and my wife and I separated. I had been so immersed in my work that I had not noticed what had been obvious to everyone else. With our marriage in ruins, my thoughts turned to my parents. My relationship with my parents, particularly with my father, had never been good, but now that they were dead I could not turn to them for help. Yet I kept writing what would eventually become this memoir of childhood. I now realize that every day I spent in their ghostly company was invisible mending; that finally I was beginning to understand, to love them and at last to see myself in them.

I WAS STANDING in my office in Trinity College, Dublin, looking out of the large window over Front Square. On the desk lay philosophy lecture notes, which I had just read over. The phone rang. The secretary told me someone wanted to speak to a philosopher. It was a few minutes before the lecture, so I asked her to send him in.

I got up, opened the door and there stood a bearded man in an old raincoat. I started – he looked just like my father. I told him to wait. After I had composed myself and showed him in, he sat down. I asked him why he wanted to speak with a philosopher and he told me he wanted to reconcile the world's religions. As he talked, scribbling notes at the same time, it soon emerged that he had the kind of mind that connects everything with everything. I was thinking how much he reminded me of Father and my eyes must have glazed over for he suddenly became irritable.

'I am the King of Heaven but it would take too long for me to explain this to you,' he shouted.

I told him I would have to leave soon. Angry now, he leaned in to my face and asked me if I even knew what he was talking about.

'I may have to kill hostages,' he said.

I froze, but did not react. This was not good.

'Do you know what I'm talking about?'

'I realize that things must be difficult for you,' I replied.

'How do you mean?'

'With your new ideas.' I was wondering how to get rid of him.

'They're not new ideas!' He was very angry now.

'Well they are your modern version of ancient ideas. I really must go downstairs now.'

To my relief, he seemed mollified by this and when I reminded him again that I had to go, we rose. At the door he told me there was no way I could contact him. I wished him good luck with a sigh of relief.

I gave the lecture but kept forgetting what to say. Ending ten minutes early, I returned to my office.

At the door I heard the phone ring. I hurried in and picked it up. It was my brother, Joss, who rang only when someone had died.

'The father's gone, this morning at ten to eight.'

After we had finished talking, I didn't feel anything. The examination bell began to ring. I had a cup of coffee, and then went off to give my next lecture.

When I returned, I rang home. Mother answered.

'We're having vegetable soup here,' she said.

'I wanted to ask how was it – at the end.'

'Well, he's gone – that's it! We're having soup now, me and your brother.'

'For Christ's sake, that's your eldest son you're talking to!' I heard my brother shout in the background.

'The funeral's soon,' she said.

WHEN I had first learned Father was ill three years earlier, Mother drove me to Larne Hospital and we entered the stone building. Our footsteps echoed along the top corridor; in the distance I could see his bearded face in a bed facing us at the end. I stepped ahead of my mother and walked up to him. His eyes widened.

'Christ, if you're here, it must be bad,' he said, looking stricken.

I felt sorry for him but at the same time I wanted to leave. Whenever I visited him and my mother, within two days I had to find some excuse to head for Dublin.

'It's good to see you,' I said.

After some initial talk of doctors' opinions, he lapsed into self-pity.

'I'm a nobody. I'm not anyone of importance.'

'You're my father, that's who you are.'

This calmed him. Now was the time to be kind. I looked out the window, filled by a large green hill, and thought of the school hymn, 'There is a green hill far away, without a city wall'.

I glanced at the man asleep in the next bed and was told it was my old headmaster at Eden village. At this he stirred and I asked him if he remembered predicting that cars of the future would run on something the size of a nut. He did and after a brief conversation between the four of us we bade Father goodbye.

When Mother and I left the ward there were tears in my eyes. As we passed the nurses' station, one remarked aloud that he would be a long time with us yet. In the car my mother was cheerful, glad even, talking all the time, for she had been relieved of the burden of nursing my father at home.

HIS ILLNESS PROGRESSED and he was put in a nursing home in Whitehead, a seaside town near my parents' Islandmagee home. After some searching, I found it in a street facing away from the sea. The home, which looked like a brick cube, stood in the shadow of pine trees grouped around it. I banged the knocker and a young nurse let me into the twilight of the hall. 'Amidst the encircling gloom,' I thought.

Inside, in a large shabby room, the inmates were gathering to have tea. My father and I stayed back on a sofa, talking.

'Come and eat, Mr Skelton,' the nurse called, but he would not join the diners. Eventually I assured him I would wait and he took a place, sitting on his own at a single table. After tea the dozen or so men and women sat in a circle; I was beside Father. The others ignored our low conversation and appeared to be resting; one or two exchanged a few words. As we talked, it became plain that he hated being there and wanted to leave. However, I also knew that my mother had said she could not cope with his illness at home. He complained that although he had rewritten *Feet Over Six* – his account of tramping through the six counties of Ulster – neither she nor I had sent the manuscript off to the publishers. This gave me an opportunity. I suggested that authors' partners were often jealous of their work. This seemed to satisfy him and slowly the conversation turned to my career.

'You've done well – I'm proud of you,' he said. Those magic words – there they were at last, but after years of waiting for them, I felt nothing. Then he began to work the conversation around to his illness. I knew he had cancer, but Mother and the doctors had decided not to tell him. I looked up; everyone around us in the circle was asleep. Then he spoke of a neighbour who had died recently, adding as an afterthought, 'but then, he had cancer'. The thought hung between us. I stayed silent. Two weeks later he was back home.

THE LAST TIME I saw my father was a year later. I had got off the train at Whitehead station and eventually found the second nursing home, a cream house with a conservatory, on the sea front. It was a quiet morning; the only sound the waves dropping on the beach, followed by the rattle of shingle.

Inside, the matron was ticking off a nurse who was standing behind a wheelchair. She turned to look at me. I asked for my father.

'Room thirteen, first floor,' she said. 'Go on up – and tell him to come down and sit in the sun.'

On the landing I glimpsed my father's back. He was sitting in an easy chair facing the light from the window.

'How are you?' I said brightly. He half-turned.

'Not the worst. Your mother was in yesterday.'

'How is she?'

'I don't think she wants me back at home.'

'Perhaps if you were nicer ...'

'Too late for me to change now. She doesn't want me there.'

I said nothing.

'Mr Skelton, Mr Skelton! Come down and get some sun.' It was the matron.

'That woman won't leave me alone.'

He stared down at his thumbs, which were resting on his thighs. We sat in silence, his clock's red second hand sweeping.

'It's too late for me. It's all too late for me now.'

'Philip Larkin said: "Sexual intercourse began in 1963 – which was rather late for me" ' I said, hoping to raise a smile, but he just glared at the wall.

'Why don't you get a bit of sun?' I asked.

'For what?'

'I have to go soon.' His face was frozen.

'Goodbye. I'll see you again, then,' I said. He did not raise his head as I left.

ON THE ISLAND, my brother Joss drove the jeep downhill to the funeral, his wife Maggie beside him. I sat in the back. Our descent ended at my parents' cottage, which was over-shadowed by the power station chimneys on the lough shore. About twenty people had gathered at Ferris Bay harbour. Backs turned to a wind off the sea between the island and Larne port; they were watching a large ferry leaving. Outside the cottage a wooden coffin sat on trestles and a little way off stood three men in RAF uniform, one bearing a flag.

'God, look at your mother!' Maggie said as we got out of the jeep. 'What a colour to wear for your husband's funeral.' My mother was dressed entirely in purple. My brother, stubbing out a cigarette in the dashboard ashtray, replied that at least she looked in good form. She was talking to the undertaker – a short, portly man in a top hat; he seemed familiar. I asked Joss if he was Billy Mahood from school, but was told he called himself William now. The man had a solemn moonface and was grasping a black umbrella at chest height just below the handle.

My mother came towards us with a smile that bordered on a grimace.

'Colour party, *halt*!' We stood watching as a wind-torn, blue flag was marched by an RAF sergeant with an officer on either side up to the coffin. I hadn't expected a military funeral for my father, though he had been a Flight Lieutenant during World War II. It seemed strange, all this pomp and ceremony outside a cottage.

Mother was shaking the hand of a clergyman. He had a scrawny neck and quick eyes.

'We'd better make a start, Alec,' she said to this cousin of my father's.

Raising one hand to the sky, the other holding a Bible to his chest, he began to speak. The group fell quiet.

'Tom and I met in the war …' The wind was blowing his words and, as he spoke, it grew dark. A passenger ship glided close behind him, blotting out the sky. Sheer sides towered over us as a bellow from its foghorn vibrated the ground under our feet. The clergyman's mouth moved in silence.

'… And Tom loved nature and he loved metaphysics …'
Far away, another foghorn called and I looked at my merchant
seaman brother.

'Did you have anything to do with this?'

He smiled.

'I thought we should give the old bastard a good send –'

'Atten…tion!' roared the colour sergeant and a trumpet
sounded 'The Last Post'. A few ex-servicemen in the gathering stood to attention. Then as the Reveille sounded, notes
bending in the wind, people began to shift and murmur.
William, the undertaker, came over.

'We'll have the coffin-bearers over here,' he called, just
loud enough to be heard over the wind. My brother and I
stepped forward. Tom, Joss's pale, teenage son, looking embarrassed, came over and asked Harry, an old airman in a beret,
where he should stand.

'Hallo, Harry. A sad day for the old soldiers,' I said.

'Indeed it is. Indeed it is. But we gave him a good show –
the Colour Party.'

'God, I'll soon be an old soldier myself. No trumpets for
me,' I laughed, referring to my own time in the RAF.

'You were never in the war,' he said, taking off his beret
and then putting it back on. I went quiet. Uncle Jack, my
father's brother, who had thick glasses, joined us and took up
the rear of the coffin with young Tom. Joss and I were at the
front; we hoisted the coffin and moved off. I thought of him
in there, my bearded father, inside that wooden box. In his
life he had always been a know-all. After he died, my mother
remarked. 'Now he really does know everything!'

On one of my visits he had been in bed and, as my daughter played on the floor, he began to talk. It was only partly

coherent, not unlike Lucky's long speech in *Waiting for Godot* – an intellectual confession, passionate but lost. He had tried this idea and hared off after that notion, but in the end had found no answers. He ended his life perplexed.

Above us on a height, framed against the big chimneys, stood the undertaker waiting for us. Arms outstretched and coat-tails flapping in the wind, he directed us with his umbrella like a farmer guiding sheep. By his demeanour he seemed to be saying: 'I am death and all of you belong to me.'

It began to rain. With the coffin stowed in the hearse, we headed over to the black limousine and, after helping my mother in beside Maggie, young Tom, Joss and I sat facing them in two foldout seats.

'Did you have to wear purple?' my brother said, 'to the father's funeral?'

' "I shall wear purple",' she began to recite as we stared, amazed, ' "with a red hat that doesn't go, and doesn't suit me. And I shall spend my pension on brandy and summer gloves …" '

She went quiet. 'Then I shall wear purple' – it's a poem, by Jenny Joseph,' she said.

The undertaker, who had been waiting under his umbrella, came over and stuck his head in the window.

'Will we go by the scenic route to the graveyard?'

We looked at my mother.

'What do you mean, the scenic route? Where's that?' she asked.

'Along the coast, so that we can remember his last journey on this earth,' the undertaker intoned.

'Stop your nonsense, Billy! Take the shortest way!' she snapped.

My brother and I exchanged looks. Tom looked shaken.

'Very well, as you wish,' the undertaker replied and the cortège set off with him at the head. As the slow journey up the hill to the graveyard began, mother drummed her fingers on the window ledge. The only other sound was the rhythm of wipers clearing rain.

'Are we nearly there yet? Is it far? Can you hurry it up,' my mother said to the driver.

'For God's sake –' said Joss.

The others were embarrassed.

'Hurry up, driver. Get a move on! We haven't got all day!' She leant forward. I looked at the driver. Impassive, he did not register even a slight smile.

'Behave yourself!' Joss snapped and she subsided in her seat.

BACK AT THE HOUSE, I started drinking and could hear my own loud laughter, which the guests politely ignored – but I felt good, knowing I should feel bad.

I went up to Father's empty bedroom while the mourners were drinking downstairs. There was something I wanted. The door was ajar and I saw a high stool in the centre of the room. On it was a parcel – his last manuscript – tied up with string and ready for posting. This one, at least, would not be rejected because no one would send it. Writers often speak of being able to paper the walls with publishers' rejection slips, but Father could have papered the ceiling too, as well as the outside of the house.

I was looking for what might be in his desk and, reaching into a drawer, drew out a few ledger-type volumes. Sitting down in the captain's chair, I checked dates. A few years seemed to be missing, but after some time I located them in various places around the room, all except 1957. The year I wanted. Perhaps he had hidden it somewhere during the forty years that had elapsed. That would make sense. The more I searched, the more convinced I became that he had hidden or even destroyed the diary for that year.

I watched from upstairs as the last mourners disappeared in ones and twos back down the hill. A bit drunk, I had gone upstairs on an impulse and was now standing beside the desk. Where could the diary be? My eye fell on a green ammunition box under the bed; it was locked. I took a screwdriver from a pot of pens and pencils on the desk and levered open the box, twisting the metal lid. There it was – a royal blue diary! I stared at it, then took it out. It fell open at April. The back cover was loose. Then I saw: all the pages from September 1957 to Christmas had been torn out – the precise period I had wanted to read about.

SOME YEARS LATER Mother too died. I had been visiting Joss, on Islandmagee at his large house overlooking the Antrim coast. We were having breakfast outside with Maggie. I was gazing up the coast and across the Irish Sea towards Scotland when Joss left the table and returned with what looked like a thick paste-in book. He handed it to me saying it was Mother's diary. I opened it at random and read what appeared to be a letter in my father's hand.

> *Dearest Fuffles,*
>
> *Just a few lines: we're on the move again. Food bloody awful – corned beef and spuds (garnished with sand), marginally better than powdered egg for breakfast I suppose. The men are longing for some leave and so am I: fat chance. Battery is running out and tent blowing down. I think of you every night and hope you will soon be safe at Sunnylands.*

I love you so very much.
Your Bof

Fuffles? Bof? I had never heard these names before but after reading several letters from my father in wartime I reached the astonishing conclusion that these were love letters – longing and passionate – astonishing, because for decades my parents had just seemed to hate each other.

I knew that my mother, Christine Mildred Knight, had come from a respectable Devon family. Her father was a banker and her mother was consumed by charity work. There were four sisters: Rachel, Grace, Doreen and my mother. Rachel, highly artistic, became matron to a boarding school and eventually died a Scientologist at the age of ninety-six in Florida. Grace became a model and married an inventor in South Africa. Doreen went to the Royal College of Art in London where she met her husband, Harold, another painter. My mother had set her heart on flower-arranging but her mother disapproved of her becoming a florist. Headstrong, she rebelled against her family's world of tea and tennis and joined the wartime RAF in 1940, where she met my father. By the age of twenty she was pregnant with me and when my father was posted abroad she had to leave for Carrick-fergus, County Antrim, to live with his parents, Ma and Pa.

For the rest of that morning I read the paste-in book and learned a great deal about those early years.

ON 10 MAY 1941 at sunrise, the Stranraer ferry from Scotland had steamed along the Antrim coast and into Larne Lough. The *Princess Victoria* had been facing into a dark sky over Belfast and was closing steadily on the quietly busy harbour of Larne. It had been a good crossing for my mother, who had only heard a single burst of machine-gun fire during the night. Her career in the Women's Royal Air Force and bid for freedom from her mother had lasted precisely seven months. When she and my father realized she was to become the mother of their child, he had applied for leave for them to get married. The Commanding Officer, a Squadron Leader Meany, not a generous man, had given them only twenty-four hours.

'Invite me to the christening,' he had said slyly, as Father left his office, furious that he had guessed they were marrying for the baby.

As the ship drew alongside the dock, she recognized her father-in-law from his photo. John Skelton, my grandfather, was a small, muscular man. That day he was wearing a blue suit and bowler hat. As she stumbled down the rickety gangway, she was grateful that he quickly came to her aid, took the large suitcase and led her to the waiting Belfast train.

Her diary notes that she saw a porter rolling milk churns, slanted on their edge, one at a time to the guard's van. The carriage jolted as, with huge slow puffs, the engine pulled the carriages out from under the wooden canopy. After passing over the narrow Larne streets, they emerged from the entrails of the seaport. The train steamed through flooded marshland filled with rotting trees and on into the countryside.

They had stopped at Whitehead, a pretty Edwardian seaside resort with the waves breaking on the sand. Like Devon, or anywhere in England in wartime, the station sign was missing, leaving instead a pair of posts. Shortly afterwards they arrived at Kilroot, Dean Swift's first parish, now a deserted Victorian brick station. One dour-looking man got off, and, wheeling his bicycle out of an archway, disappeared.

Next, the train moved slowly past a strange structure, resembling a small station. It was, in fact, a rusty corrugated iron hut on top of a kind of platform made of cinders and railway sleepers. There was no nameplate there either. This was Eden village. Behind the hut, in the far distance across the sea, was a large Norman castle.

They got off in view of the castle at Carrickfergus and, slipping through a hole in the hedge, started up a cinder avenue. They then passed through a barbed-wire military enclosure where she got a few wolf-whistles from the Canadian soldiers stationed there. Halfway up the avenue, my grandfather had to help round up some cattle and Mother went on ahead, walking towards the wooded end of the path.

In years to come, my mother never tired of telling of her reception at Sunnylands House. As she passed through the trees, she saw, on the right of the swerving avenue, a handsome ivy-covered house and, on her left, a large overgrown lawn. She approached what appeared to be the front door, in a conservatory, and pressed the ceramic button set in a dull brass surround. A bell rang far away in the house. She turned to look around and saw, some distance away, a dark figure in a hat, hunched in a wheelchair, watching her from behind horn-rimmed glasses. She was surprised at this imposing house and thought my father had exaggerated his humble origins. No one came to the door; she rang again, longer this time. Presently, through the glass, she saw a tall, thin woman in tweeds appear. She looked annoyed at being disturbed.

'Mrs Skelton? I'm Christine,' she had said.

'They're round the back,' the woman said. 'Go round to the back door!'

Blushing, my mother continued on round the side of the house. At home, her own mother would never even speak to a servant like that.

At the back door she got a warm welcome from her mother-in-law. Ma, a handsome imperious woman with a strong Ulster accent, introduced her to her new sister-in-law. About her own age, Sadie was working in the scullery, scrubbing potatoes over a large white rectangular sink. A brass tap was running while a Primus stove quietly roared on the draining board.

As they left the scullery, my mother had noticed long cracks in the wall from floor to ceiling, but, on entering the kitchen she felt a strong feeling of homeliness. Facing her was a big black range; there was a red glow from the grate on the right. Above it was a generous mantelpiece with a large carriage clock in the middle. At either end tall figurines held torches aloft, on the left '*Le Jour*', on the right '*La Nuit*'. There was a framed black and white photograph of a yacht and she was told that was *The Scamp*, with which Pa had won so many cups. Her eye lit on a magnificent silver rose bowl in the centre of a polished table.

After tea, Sadie led her from the tiled kitchen into the scullery and brought her on a tour of the house. She was shown the solid wooden door of the pantry, Pa's workshop, and then they passed a large dark space around the bottom of a long staircase. This, she was told, had been the billiard room. At the foot of the stairs were large oblong shapes covered in dustsheets. There was a crumbling harpsichord and a piano. She began idly playing the scale with one hand and Sadie was delighted they had the piano in common.

She found that her bedroom overlooked a farmyard. On the wall was a small picture of Highland cattle grazing in some Scottish glen; the hills were purple. On a Victorian washstand was a floral jug and basin. There was also a candlestick with a half-burned white candle. The candlestick was encrusted with dry melted wax. It had slowly dawned on her … no electricity.

Ma's room had a brass bedstead with one of its pear-shaped knobs at a queer angle. The bed itself was beside a large window which had a small hole in the middle, plugged by a wad of paper. Three long cracks spread from the hole to the far edges of the window frame, beside which was a bedside table crammed with medicines.

Pa slept in an adjoining narrow room and what caught her attention was an open trunk half full of coins. She noted it was like a pirate's sea chest. Sadie told her it was the rents which Pa collected around the town for a solicitor.

Outside the house she came upon Pa's yacht in the byre and met Dash, his red setter gundog, who slept in the stable. Mother asked about the man in the wheelchair and was told that he and his wife, the Bates, rented the front of the house. She learned that Pa was only the caretaker and that he and his family had lived there rent-free for thirty years, ever since the owner had gone to Australia. Mr Bates was the brother of Sir Dawson Bates, a government minister, and therefore they could not be expected to live in the back of the house. She also found out that there had been a row years before: Pa had borrowed the Bates' new axe and had lost it.

In the middle of the day she noted they ate something called 'champ' – mashed potato with chopped scallions and a lump of butter in the middle. It was washed down with tea. She had found it comforting and slept a little afterwards.

At four there was no cup of tea, like at home, but later Pa lit the oil lamp on the polished kitchen table and at six they had the evening meal called 'tea' – it was cheese on toast. Then Sadie played piano while my mother read by the lamp, thinking how romantic it all was and got ready for an early night.

Sadie handed her a candlestick with a loop handle – just like the ones in children's stories. She said goodnight to Ma and Pa, then started up the long staircase. Halfway up, the candle flame guttered, there was a sudden noise. She hesitated. Suddenly the piano rang out in the blackness. Haphazard notes going up the keyboard, then down. Silence. She froze;

the flame blew out. Sadie called down the stairs that it was only the mice in the piano.

Her bedroom door was open and there was a candlestick on the bedside table. She undressed and, folding her clothes neatly on the chair, knelt in prayer for a few seconds, then got into bed. It smelt musty and was cold but her feet found a stone hot water jar.

ON HER FIRST MORNING at Sunnylands she was woken at six by two cocks crowing in ragged unison. Then she went back to sleep until nine. Out of bed, she washed in cold water from the floral jug on the dressing table and went down to breakfast. Ma sat at a large square polished table beside a tall oil lamp looking out at the hens in the large farmyard. Sadie was frying breakfast on the range.

They all sat at the big table with the large silver rose bowl in the middle. Ma poured tea for my mother, who blanched at how dark it was – even after milk.

'For God's sake you could trot a horse on that tea – give her some milk,' Sadie had said. When my mother tasted the eggs and bacon, she pronounced this the best breakfast ever.

Pa didn't seem to do anything except cut wood and shoot hares and plover in the fields that lay around. She soon discovered that to a considerable extent the Skeltons lived off the land. Sadie had asked her to come up the garden to get potatoes. Pa accompanied them and they watched while Sadie dug them up. She thought it was like magic, how perfectly formed purple potatoes came up out of the dark earth with the turn of the garden fork. Pa picked them out and filled her basket, for, being pregnant, bending down was too hard for her now. She liked Pa – he was kind – but she wasn't sure about Ma. Only that morning she had been trying to light the methylated spirits in the little tray in the Primus stove. It was difficult and the match kept going out. Aware someone was looking, she glanced up to see Ma watching her efforts without offering to help.

Sadie soon taught her what she needed to learn and she became accustomed to washing potatoes and chopping vegetables, to accompany whatever Pa could shoot for the pot; mostly rabbit. As a girl, she had kept a pet rabbit in a neat hutch at the bottom of the garden, but now, when doing the washing up, she often turned round to stare at a rabbit hanging head down on the back door. For some reason they always had blood on their teeth.

Her life, like Sadie's, was now revolving around the range, preparing and cooking broth. Since they had piano in common, the two young women got on well. Sadie, the primary school teacher, regaled her with tales of the classroom at the Knockagh school to which she cycled uphill, three miles every morning. She had a reputation for being tough but fair. In later years I met one of her ex-pupils, who remarked: 'the softest part of that woman was her teeth'. But Sadie had her vulnerable side, for she was very keen on a man called Afie and would often cycle up to the Blahole, a windy spot above Whitehead where young people gathered, in the hope of meeting him. But Afie seemed uninterested and on the rebound she began dating a soldier stationed at the camp down the avenue.

During this period of the pregnancy, Mother occupied her evenings writing and pasting in topical clippings from the papers to make a diary-cum-scrapbook. One entry shows on the left page a photograph of a young woman scrubbing a floor on her hands and knees. On the facing page is a ballerina resting on the floor. The two young women are kneeling in the same way: on the left the ballerina, on the right the skivvy. It was clear Mother had been contrasting what she had once dreamed of being with what she felt she had now become. Odd memories occur in the diary too, like the day she got soaked in Belfast buying a Gor-Ray skirt, but mostly it was about missing dear Bof and longing for letters that often didn't arrive.

The German bombers, en route to Belfast, always woke her at three in the morning. One night, after their engine noise had died away, she sat up in bed and wrote: 'I hope our son has a true Irish voice, deep and grand but quick as one of their reels.'

I came a few days early; her waters had broken in the early evening after tea at six. Pa was sitting reading the *News Letter* by the fire; Sadie was reading a magazine and Ma was sewing. Mother felt something shift inside her and told Ma, who told Pa to go for nurse G.

After they cycled back together, Pa settled downstairs, reading the paper by the range. There he sat while Sadie, Ma and the nurse came and went, giving him bulletins on the candlelit birth, which had not begun until three in the morning. At dawn, my mother told me, I came into the world to the ragged crowing of the two cocks and the dawn chorus.

Nurse G pronounced me a hefty infant and since I had started bawling, remarked on my lusty lungs. She began washing me in a shallow bowl, as Mother lay back exhausted, listening to water run off my skin and back into the bowl. The birdsong died away gradually and soon she was holding me and looking into my eyes as the morning sun lit the walls of the room. Eleven days later, there was an air raid and we all had to go downstairs. My mother wrote how she sat with Pa, Ma and Sadie, who held me as they huddled together under the staircase with the bombers roaring over the house.

From early on, Ma always liked to wheel my pram and, as I grew, she would often pick me up. But what annoyed Mother most was that, as time wore on, Ma took me into her bed in the morning. One day she woke and, finding me gone, rushed to Ma's room: there she found us sitting up in bed together. Ma was feeding me with a teaspoon. But it was the way I looked over at her, she wrote, as if to say: who are you? She felt defeated by Ma and determined to leave. And she did. For the remainder of the war she and I lived with her sister Doreen in Surrey. Later we moved to a caravan behind a pub at Trodds Lane in Surrey where Mother helped in the bar.

My main memory from that time was a rare visit from Father, who put me out to play while presumably he and Mother spent some time alone together. While I was playing outside, a pig burst through the hedge and my cries brought Father rushing out to see what was wrong. He just laughed and Mother picked me up. Another time the publican, who was cutting the hedge with a billhook, let me, a five-year-old, have a go and I promptly cut my finger to the bone. Mother seems to have been very angry about this but as the Allied victory was imminent, we went back to Sunnylands to await Father's return from the war.

One day Mother was in the scullery at Sunnylands when there was a knock at the door. Outside stood a man in uniform and, without waiting to look at him or ask what he wanted, called back over her shoulder to Sadie that it was just another soldier looking for water.

'You bloody fool, it's me!' the soldier had snapped. It was my father, so sunburnt and emaciated that she had not recognized him.

When I saw him, apparently I opened my mouth and bawled for I had no idea who this stranger was. He, in his turn, no doubt traumatized by war, was perplexed by my reaction and probably felt helpless. In retrospect, it seems that on the day of Father's return, our relationship had got off on the wrong foot.

FROM THE AGES of five to nine I slept and woke to the sound of the river at the bottom of our garden. We were living in a semi-detached brick house at Trooperslane, a small hamlet under the Knockagh hill.

The house had already assumed a place in the family folklore. Pa had inherited the house from his two schoolteacher sisters, Sissy and Maggie. Sissy, who taught at the industrial school in York Street, Belfast, was said to have been a stickler for grammar. Maggie was a matron in the same school. But the sisters were celebrated for another reason. One day a bull had crashed through their hedge into the back garden. Undaunted, the sisters had seized umbrellas and, opening and closing them, had advanced on the puzzled beast. It had slowly turned and lumbered back to the field, defeated. They also kept hidden behind the dresser a prized copy of *Moore's*

Melodies – hidden because in those days such crossing of traditions was not common. After they had gone to live in Donaghadee, where they died, my Uncle Jack had moved in with his new wife, Betty.

Betty was a beauty from a local influential family of doctors and lawyers, the Loughridges, who did not approve of the marriage. At that time Jack had opened a shop in the Shankill Road, a very Protestant, poor area in Belfast. Partly because Betty was unwilling to work in the shop, the business did not do well, so that when the Loughridge family would not help, Jack had to turn to his own father, Pa, for money. When my cousin Sandra was born, Mrs Loughridge would not recognize her grand-daughter for over a year until, under social pressure, she finally relented. Jack ended up working for his father-in-law, a successful builder, and was effectively in his wife's family's pocket for life. Neither could Betty escape their tentacles for, even in death, she made sure that her gravestone was inscribed with her maiden name: Betty Loughridge.

In our house, I was awoken each morning by Father going to his study to write. Only when I heard Mother moving about, would I get up, dress and go downstairs into the red-tiled kitchen where she gave me pieces of bread. Then out through the porch to place the food on the bird table and stand there among the gardens of Trooperslane. There were six double houses, in one of which lived Uncle Jack, Betty and their daughter, Sandra. At the house farthest up the hill lived Commander Allworth, who gave cocktail parties to which my parents were sometimes invited.

High over Trooperslane presided the Knockagh monument. This tall stone obelisk, a replica of the Wellington monument in Dublin's Phoenix Park, was a memorial to the fallen of World War I. On fine summer mornings, it stood in sharp relief against the blue sky. Mother and I would walk down the garden path and stand on the wooden bridge over the river at the front gate.

Close by was the railway station and, hearing a clank, we would see Andy, the stationmaster, close the railway gates across our road for the first train of the day. As we stood watching the bird table, the air was filled with river sounds from under our feet. Mostly sparrows came to feed, but whenever a greenfinch or a goldfinch landed, my mother would stand beaming until it flew off, and then we would go inside for breakfast.

For the first year we lived off Father's RAF gratuity. Each day he sat upstairs in his study reading, writing and, most of all, typing. In those years I had no idea what it meant to be in a war and it was not until long after his death that I had any appreciation of what he had been through.

I discovered some of his early manuscripts in my brother's attic and his harrowing experiences came home to me. Reading the dusty typewritten sheets, I was shaken to learn that he had managed to get through battles only by assuming he was already dead. I also realized that he had spent so long pretending to be dead, or assuming he was already dead, that after the war he had found it difficult to rejoin the living. One manuscript was a short memoir about the Allied advance up through Italy, with the Germans in retreat. Their path was filled with charred vehicles, bomb craters and dead bodies, but there was a single numinous moment.

One afternoon he had taken a walk away from battle and gone down a quiet road at the side of an orchard. He had sauntered along for some time enjoying the tranquillity and eventually came to a village untouched by war. He stopped and stared. A beautiful young woman came out of a doorway and, crossing the empty street, seemed to sense his eyes on her. She turned and looked provocatively at him: he stood there stunned. Then she vanished, leaving him in wonder at the vision he had just experienced in that quiet Italian village. Afterwards as they moved through Italy he wrote that he had begun to dare to feel more alive. However, the habit of being dead, I believe, never left him.

Father had not joined the Royal Air Force to fight the war, nor had he been enlisted, for there was no conscription in Ulster. He had joined because he was unemployed. When he had left 'Inst', the well-established Belfast grammar school to which he had won a scholarship, he had become an apprentice bookseller. At the same time, Father preached the Gospel in the streets of Carrickfergus.

Ma had her heart set on him going into the Church, but disapproved of street preaching. The family story was that there had been no money to send him to university but the real reason may have been different. Since he found her so overbearing, he may have just refused to do what she wanted. She often told the story that, as a boy, he had once become so angry with her that he had taken his two younger brothers, together with Sadie, one by one, high up into the tallest tree in the wood. Ma apparently nearly had heart failure when, looking up, she saw them all sitting along a branch fifty feet from the ground.

Father soon tired of bookselling and expressed a wish to work in a leper colony. Instead, to his parent's great relief, he joined the RAF as a clerk. Shortly afterwards, war broke out and he had stayed for the duration of the conflict.

Father was the eldest of four children. His brother, Sammy, fought in the war, was captured by the Japanese, but escaped. Jack stayed at home and Sadie became a teacher. Their young lives had been spent on the Sunnylands estate and down at Carrick boathouse, sailing or swimming. They had the run of the big house and often played football in the ballroom, but when the Bates arrived they retreated to the back of the house. One incident from his childhood preoccupied my father – that as a boy he had been made to help Pa carry the boom of his yacht up through the town. Around the boom was the sail and inside that were hidden two or three rifles. With Pa at the front and his son at the rear, they often had to pass a policeman. At such times, my father said, he prayed and prayed that if they were not caught he would never break the law again. All my life he was law-abiding to a fault and would become furious if, for example, I had no bell on my bike.

Each morning as Father began writing, my mother walked me two miles to the Model School in Carrickfergus. As I sat down in class, Miss Hawkins would pull one end of the piano out from the wall and reach down behind it. She would emerge a moment later waving aloft the large, multiple mousetrap, mice tails and bodies dangling in the air.

'Look children: five today!'

Then, releasing the dead mice on to the flames of the coal fire, she would lay the trap on the piano and sit down to play the introduction to our morning hymn.

> Yes, Jesus loves me,
> Yes, Jesus loves me,
> Yes, Jesus loves me,
> The Bible tells me so.

UNLIKE OUR Presbyterian neighbours, including Uncle Jack, my father did not go to church and the Bible was not mentioned much at home. There was more discussion about the football pools, from which my parents hoped to win a fortune. Every Saturday evening they listened to the radio and bent to the task of checking their soccer match predictions. Waiting for the results on Saturday evenings made them so tense, Father finally called an end to the football pools. Another dream they had was a paid ticket to Australia, but since my father had no trade or profession this never happened.

So now he wrote and wrote upstairs while downstairs my mother would play Dvorak's Slavonic Dances on the piano. When I sat on the stairs, I was between the clack clack of the typewriter above and my mother's piano playing below. Whenever he took a break from writing, my father tended the bees in the back garden: three hives painted red, white and blue respectively. At other times he took Sassy, a black labrador, for a walk across the fields. She was a sweet-tempered dog who had only one weakness. It turned out that a neighbour, who was having milk stolen, had got up early to keep watch. Sassy, she said, came up the path, approached the milk bottles, tipped them over with one paw, punctured the top with her teeth and drank all the milk.

Sometimes Father got together with writers in Belfast like Sam Hanna Bell and John Boyd, but he was particularly respectful of Louis MacNeice, a poet of some distinction. So when the poet acquired a borzoi, a Russian wolfhound, Mother encouraged my father to get one too. This aristocratic, otherworldly, long-haired creature was christened Natasha and for the most part she got on well with the homely Sassy.

The pair accompanied the three of us on our walks over the fields or up Knockagh Hill on Sundays.

During these walks my mother gathered flowers and twigs, for her great love was arranging flowers and she often repeated the tale that she had left home because her mother would not let her pursue it as a career. At odd moments in the evenings, she sketched or modelled in clay and at bedtime she always read to me. One favourite was Longfellow's *Hiawatha*: 'By the shores of Gitche Gumee / By the shining Big-Sea-Water, / Stood the wigwam of Nokomis, / Daughter of the Moon, Nokomis.'

The Reverend MacNeice, the poet's father, had been a prominent figure in Carrickfergus as, head held high, he went about parish business. His son, Louis, appeared in the town on vacations from his school in England. Twenty years later, he was to become a mentor to my father, putting in a word for him at BBC Northern Ireland, as it then was, enabling him to broadcast on country life. So, the poet had, in an erratic way, become father's occasional companion; erratic because the poet drank so much that there was no telling if, or when, he would turn up. Possibly MacNeice felt he could identify with this struggling writer from his own home town. I subsequently came to feel that because of MacNeice's English education, an essential part of his Irishness had been left back in Ulster and, in his mind, an element of that was my father.

Twice a week, Mrs Hannah came to clean and her sunny presence cheered us all. If my father were out walking, she would take the opportunity to tidy his study. One day he returned to find his typewriter in a pool of water on the desk.

'Mary, could you come here a minute?' he called downstairs. She arrived puffing on to the landing.

'What in the name of God has happened here?'

'Oh, the machine looked dirty, so I boiled it to make it really clean,' she said.

My father let the matter drop but later, when it had dried off, he squirted bicycle oil into the mechanism. It worked well from then on. But he never forgot the incident and would tell and retell the story.

When I was seven, one summer evening my parents and I were out over the fields with the dogs. I had been asking Father about the war for some time now but he had always refused to talk about it. I asked him again but still he did not reply, yet to my astonishment he ran forward, did two somersaults, ran again, swerved and did another somersault. A bit out of breath, he told me it was part of his job in the war to teach soldiers how to avoid being shot. I asked him to do it again, but he would not. On future walks, when he thought I wasn't looking, he would suddenly do it, and then refuse to repeat the performance.

We often walked over the fields on summer evenings. On the way home on one occasion he and I lagged behind my mother and, for a joke, he tried to persuade me to hide from her in some gorse bushes. I cried so much that he had to give up and allowed me to run back to her.

She was scornful about my father's attempt to win me over; in his own way he was probably trying to get me on his side, having seen that during the war I had become over-attached to her and also to Ma.

When Mother became pregnant again he had less and less time for me and soon the walks drew to a close. Now I found Mother preoccupied and short-tempered.

'How dare you! How dare you!' she shouted at me, and

then left me crying on the landing outside Father's brown-varnished study door. It opened. Surprised, I stopped crying, allowed myself to be picked up, taken inside and put up on his knee. I examined his stubble; he smelt of tobacco.

'Will I tell you a story?'

I nodded and he slowly began building a story about the first Red Indian until we were both caught up in the yarn. When it was over, he returned me, happy, to my mother, who had calmed down.

At weekends my parents did gardening, but it was hard, for the ground was red clay and little grew in it. Pegged in a corner of the lawn was a seed packet showing a coloured picture of magnificent lupin blooms, but our seeds never grew. Once my father found what he called a chrysalis in the garden. It was an ordinary brown capsule and he said that if we kept it warm indoors it would hatch into a beautiful butterfly. He put it inside a Perspex box and placed it on the mantelpiece. Each day I examined it for signs of life, but it remained the same brown capsule, day in day out. I thought it would somehow be like the first Red Indian story, which had seemed to come from nowhere. But eventually, slowly, my hopes of seeing a coloured butterfly emerge faded.

After a year my father's gratuity began to run out. He had published almost nothing and we had little money. Mrs Hannah had to be let go. When my parents told her, she offered to work for nothing, but they couldn't agree to that, saying that it was unfair to her. My father started applying for jobs advertised in the papers and after some time secured a civil service post in Belfast.

During the pregnancy, visits to the doctor, or as my parents insisted on calling him, the Quack, were quite frequent. Dr

Loughridge's surgery was near Kelly's coal office, which faced Carrick Castle. When Mother went in to pay the coal bill, I studied the models of the coal boats in glass cases. Then we walked along the street on the seafront and entered the surgery through a red-tiled porch doorway.

The Loughridges' dining room served as a waiting room. It had a large polished table in the centre. There was a huge silver bowl of red and yellow roses, which were reflected deep in the surface of the table.

Presently the Quack would come in. He always wore a pressed grey suit, which matched his neat grey hair parted on one side. But it was his voice that struck me. It had a strange metallic quality like the Tin Man in *The Wizard of Oz*. I later learned it was because he was tone deaf. My mother would rise and I would hear their muffled voices until the surgery door closed. Then I was alone.

I would sit in the silence staring at the white light filtering through the net curtains on the sea-facing windows. Occasionally a horse and cart plodded and jingled past the windows, the dark shape blurred by the fabric. Sometimes I got up and gazed through the muslin where I could just make out the dark outline of the castle. Father said it had the ghost of a white rabbit living down a well. How could a rabbit live down a well? Alice had fallen down a well into Wonderland, passing all the shelves as she fell. And there had been the white rabbit with a pocket watch. The noise of another cart jingling past, going the other way, would wake me from my reverie. Filtered through the curtain fabric, suspended in the air, the dark, white shapes of seagulls loomed.

The day came, as it did for all children then, when Dr Loughridge told Mother that my tonsils had to be taken out.

My friend, Mark McIlroy, had to have his out too, so our mothers arranged for us to go at the same time and share a room.

When I woke after the operation, my throat was dry and tasted of blood; there was crying somewhere and, levering myself up in the bed, I looked towards the noise. It was coming from a new cot, which had been moved into the room. In it was a small boy who screamed and cried while trying to climb up out of the cot.

I tried to speak to the nurse, but she left the room.

'I wish they'd take him away,' said Mark in the next bed.

We drifted back into a twilight state with the awful noise still going on when suddenly there was a crash. The small boy in the cot, which was more like a cage, had climbed over the rail and had fallen on the floor. We watched as two nurses, using long bandages, secured the wild boy down inside his cot. Now he was tied to the bars. At last he fell quiet. Relieved, I lay back in peace for a while, and then sat up to drink some water. I smelled something.

Mark and I propped ourselves up on our elbows. The tethered boy had started shitting. It was all over his legs and the brown bandages sawed into his excrement-covered legs. The screaming started again as he struggled to escape. Finally a nurse came in and, leaning back into the corridor, shouted: 'Doris, give us a hand with this one, will you?' They wheeled out the cot cage with its screaming, brown-smeared prisoner. We never saw him again.

The next day Mark's mother came for him, leaving me on my own in the room. I whiled away the morning playing with a Dinky taxi and looking out of the window at the Belfast traffic below. My mother was coming to fetch me at one o'clock and everything was packed and ready. I sat on the side of the bed to wait for her and after a while a nurse came in – the one called Doris.

'What're you waiting for?' she chirped.

'My mummy's coming for me,' I said. She went out and after ten minutes came back. She looked amused.

'Still waiting? Maybe she's not coming.'

I must have gone white.

'Maybe she will,' she said hastily, but it was too late: the seed had been planted.

As one o'clock gave way to two o'clock, I listened less carefully to the sound of the footsteps in the polished corridor. When my mother dashed in breathless at twenty past two, I hardly noticed. Later she told me she had found me sitting silently like a little old man on the side of the bed. She asked me what was wrong.

'They said you weren't coming,' I whispered.

'Who said?'

'Her,' I said, pointing to the nurse who was entering the room.

'Did you tell him I wasn't coming?' said Mother, blushing with anger.

'I was only joking,' said the nurse before skittering quickly out.

EACH DAY my father caught the train from beside our house to his civil service office job in Belfast. He wore his 'uniform' of sports jacket and flannels and, although my mother knew he still missed the action of war and the open air, she looked at him with pride each morning as he went off to work. When he came home in the evening, he would bring balsa wood to make model planes and a strong-smelling substance called dope to paint the wings.

The aeroplane interest had started by a fluke. One Sunday morning my mother was gardening; I was indoors playing and my father was upstairs in his study.

'Tom, Tom, come quickly!' my mother called excitedly. We ran outside. There on the grass was a large model plane with a four-foot wingspan. We marvelled at it and, while we were wondering where it had come from, there was a hammering at the front door.

Outside was a small man who could scarcely speak from panting. The plane was his, he said, and he had pursued it across the fields. When he had calmed down, he had tea and began to talk about his hobby with great enthusiasm. My father couldn't get enough of it. The next Monday he came home from Belfast armed with strips of balsa wood and embarked on another of his 'crazes'.

From then on, at the weekends, he would sit down with me and build a model aeroplane. I handed him the parts and he did the building, slicing the soft wood with a razor blade and gluing pieces together. The powerful smell enveloped the kitchen. He found the fiddly work irritating and the whole thing put him in a bad temper. But the worst aspect of it was that when a new plane of ours was flown in the field behind our house, he would loudly proclaim to the few spectators that I had built it. I wished he wouldn't do that for I had actually made only a small part of it.

At that time I was fascinated by glimpses I had of him shaving in the mornings. One evening lying awake in bed, I could no longer contain my curiosity about shaving and took his packet of razor blades from the bathroom. In bed, I started to unwrap them one by one and, dimly aware that my fingers were becoming sticky, fell asleep. I was awakened in the morning by screaming and shaking, Mother had come in to wake me and found blood and razor blades all over the pillow. Father came up to see what was wrong.

'Didn't I tell you not to leave those razor blades around?' she raged. I savoured his crestfallen look.

My father continued to write for a while in the evenings after dinner but when he stopped, he either sat staring, or flew into a fury at the smallest thing. At night he often shouted out from nightmares, which my mother said came from the war. During the Allied advance through Italy, he had contracted malaria from a mosquito bite. When the condition recurred, I sometimes peered into the smelly, darkened bedroom, where he would be sweating and raving in a delirium. This would continue for several days, after which he would return to normal.

My parents often bickered over breakfast, but one morning my mother had accused him of not inviting her to an office function where she had heard that he had been dancing with one of the secretaries.

'Grounds for divorce! Grounds for divorce!' she joked but with a serious edge. I sat silent, apparently not listening. Cross, he went upstairs.

'I hate him. I don't love him,' she declared.

Shortly afterwards, he came down.

'Mummy says she doesn't love you.'

He didn't say anything. I was embarrassed.

'I never said that!' she said, going red. My father said he had to go and, reluctantly, she brushed his jacket before he went to the train, with no further word.

ON SATURDAY AFTERNOONS we were often in the front garden. One day my parents were reading the newspapers while I lay on my tummy, staring deep into Sassy's eyes. Classical music was drifting out of the front window from the wireless and the river could be heard intermittently. Sassy gave a single *wuff* into my face. I wiped the saliva off my cheek. She growled suddenly.

'What's that? Could you turn off the radio, Millie?' Father said and sat up as she went inside the house. I could hear nothing. The radio stopped and just as she returned, we heard a flute.

'It's Sam Erskine by God. He said he'd be back this way,' said my father, excited.

'Really, darling,' said Mother watching Natasha, who was growling. We stood up on the lawn as a tramp came marching up the hill and over the open gates of the railway crossing. He wore a flat cap and marched slightly bowed, flute to one side. We gathered on the bridge at the gate and, as he came up, I saw that one of his eyes stayed still all the time.

'Well, Sam, you're a sight for sore eyes,' my father called out, opening the front gate and shaking the man's hand.

'Will you have cup of tea?' said Mother, gingerly offering him her hand.

'I would Missus, I would.'

She disappeared into the house as Father waved him to the deckchair he had just vacated.

'Have you come far today, Sam?'

'About fifteen mile,' said the tramp.

Eventually, Mother returned with a tray and poured tea. I couldn't stop staring at the eye that didn't move.

'Your boy's interested in the glass eye,' he said through a mouthful of biscuits. 'Tom, did I ever tell you about the time I was on the building site and the foreman – I can't recall the name – said: "Samuel," says he, "would you run your eye along that wall and see if it's straight?"

' "Right you are," I said.' At this point, the tramp put his hand to his face and the glass eye appeared between his fingers. He held it like a marble.

'And I scooted it like a marble, along the top of the wall and, Tom, that foreman turned his back and was sick.'

They laughed. I could not take my eyes off the empty red eye socket and started to cry.

'Come on, we'll go inside,' said Mother.

Sam Erskine stayed that night. He and Father sat on either side of the fireplace as the stranger read aloud his poetry. I was allowed to stay up a little longer and sat on a small stool beside my mother, watching.

'By God, Sam, that's marvellous!' my father said, but my mother, displaced from her usual chair by the fire, sat in the background, uninterested. I didn't like the man's bad smell but we liked it when he took out his flute and played. Surprised at the way his music flowed, my mother, on her way to the kitchen, danced a few steps.

As the evening wore on, he and Father had a few glasses

of whiskey and became quite merry. The hobo conjured a picture of himself tramping a country road playing the flute as he went and this excited my father, but Mother just looked worried.

Aside from the flute, Mother made it obvious that she didn't much care for the stranger and doused the mattress he had slept on with DDT powder as she waited for him to leave. Natasha would not even go near the tramp. It was with great relief Mother and I said goodbye to him on the Sunday morning.

'I'll go part of the road with him. Expect me back for lunch.' Father said, holding the borzoi by the collar.

When they had gone, Mother could hardly wait to get his mattress out of the house. She and I struggled with it down the stairs and out the back door, where we left it against the hedge. Then, using Jeyes Fluid, she scrubbed the study where he had slept, which left another stink in Father's den. By lunchtime she was exhausted and made us baked beans on toast. Afterwards we went out to the garden and I read a Rupert Bear comic book with Sassy alongside. Mother fell asleep.

She woke in the deckchair at half past four when Sassy began licking her face. Then, pushing the dog back, she looked at her watch.

'Where's your father got to? He should have been back by now,' she said.

'I'm going to phone. Come on.' She got up. We walked up the road towards the grass triangle at the top. Children were playing there, shouting and screaming in the fading light. We turned into the Allworth's house by the triangle to ask to use the phone. My parents no longer visited this house; they had once attended cocktail parties there but invitations had tailed off, probably because of Father's outspoken manner.

'Millie, I'm afraid the telephone's broken,' said Mrs All-worth, 'What's wrong, my dear? You look upset.'

'It's Tom – he's not back and it's getting dark.'

'Yes, he passed the house talking with some tramp earlier. I thought he was escorting him away from the area.' She pursed her lips and looked away. 'Sorry, I can't help,' she said as we turned to go. At the gate I could hear the telephone ring back in the house.

We went out to the road and walked downhill in the dusk. Now my mother would ask Andy at the railway station to use the phone. He was whistling between his teeth as he closed the railway gates to trains for the night.

'Andy, it's Tom. I have to phone the police. He's not back yet and it's nearly dark!'

Andy stopped whistling, turned round, glanced at her tearful face, then gazed up at the darkening hill.

'Isn't that him there?' he said, pointing.

'Thank goodness,' she said, running back across the rails and up the hill towards Father.

'Where were you?' she demanded. 'I was sick with worry.' My father seemed impervious. He looked happy, even excited.

'Sorry. I forgot the time,' he said.

IT WAS soon after this that Father got a noisy motorbike and sidecar. My mother hated it but he enjoyed riding at high speed, hair flying, wearing aviation goggles. It reminded him, he said, of the Indian motorbike he had ridden in the North Africa desert war. About this time, too, he left his desk job and got a new one that I did not understand. Each night he came home from the new job with his motorbike and hobnail boots covered in clay. My mother said he had a job building the new factory, Courtaulds, at Carrickfergus and was very tired because he had to dig holes in the ground all day. He did not speak much any more but I remember his enthusiasm about his 'black can' – a tin with a wire handle used for brewing tea over a fire on the site. This had been blackened over the fire at home so that he would not stick out among the other navvies.

Before long he stopped shaving and grew a beard. For his mother, Ma, this was the mark of the artisan and she would no longer speak to him. And, because of the long hours and overtime, his temper was short and by Christmas I had become wary of being near him.

ON BOXING DAY morning my parents were having a rare lie-in. I was playing with my toy crane, occasionally glancing out at a light snowfall. The crane had come from Santa and its delivery had woken me in the dark. The next morning Mother had some explaining to do as I quizzed her about Santa and whether or not he existed. She replied that of course he existed – hadn't my father actually seen him in the snow as his reindeer and sleigh swept round the corner of our road and continued up the hill. I could immediately believe this picture, which was never to leave me.

As the morning wore on, I became more and more hungry. I knocked on their brown door; there was a muffled conver-sation and a thump as someone got out of bed. Almost imme-diately the door opened: my bearded father was wearing only a vest, under which something was sticking up. Just below the vest an ugly-looking hairy sac hung down.

'I don't want you. I want Mummy,' I said. He hit me twice. My mother protested, but her voice was drowned out by a flurry of slapping until, in shock and tears, I retreated to my room. Nothing like this had ever happened before.

FATHER NOW EMBARKED on a kind of diary, which was to become his memoir, *Clay Under Clover*. Despite the exhaustion from his labouring work, he wrote every evening after I had gone to bed. He always used the same pen, a Parker 51, of which he was very proud.

When I was upstairs in bed, I could hear my parents' muffled voices and would picture them on either side of the fire. Sometimes in the mornings I found my mother had fashioned model animals from the red clay from the garden – the same clay my father dug for a living at work on the new factory across the fields from Trooperslane. She also began designing a jersey for him on graph paper and then spent most of a winter knitting it. Across the back was a picture of the Carrickfergus skyline with the town's castle in the centre; across the chest were portraits of Sassy and Natasha together with a pick, a shovel and a walking stick.

Mother was also Father's typist and when I got back from school she would be struggling to read his minuscule handwriting, often having to guess what he had written. Before long there was a sizeable typescript, a kind of diary of my civil servant father's initiation into the world of the navvy.

ONE SUMMER SATURDAY he came home excited and I heard him tell my mother he had bumped into someone in Belfast's Royal Avenue. 'I met Louis in town and he wants to come down and have a look at the book tomorrow.'

'That's marvellous, darling.'

When Louis MacNeice arrived, Father and he, lying back in deck chairs, had tea in the garden. Natasha lay by the visitor and the poet occasionally petted her. Later my mother, who was heavily pregnant, joined us and sat back on a chair reading the paper while I lay on the grass beside Sassy.

Father had handed the poet a sheaf of typewritten pages, and then had lit a cigarette and sat back. I watched as the poet shuffled the paper. Bored, I stared deep into the grass where insects were crawling among gigantic stalks of grass. Eventually he stopped reading; my father looked worried.

'I like this bit, Tam.' He had a metallic, flat voice.

' "Even there, down in a deep hole, looking up I can see, on a good day, the pale-blue sky roofing the walls of the hole. The man who looks up can only see the sky; the man who looks down can only see the hole. I do not suggest there is very much beauty in a hole, unless it be in the precision-trimmed sides; but a clay hole is a strangely homely place." Lovely, that's great stuff, and this bit here, where you have to clear the trees: "The sun shone down, I thought angrily, on the scene, which was disorder. Trees were lying where they had been trailed over the grass, with their black roots pointing dark fingers into a blue sky." '

'I think it'll be a great book,' pronounced the poet as Father sat silent. 'Why don't you send it to a publisher? Gollancz might like it.'

SOME MONTHS LATER Mother and I were doing the washing up when my father came in the kitchen looking dazed. He silently passed her a letter. She dried her hands on the apron and took it.

'That's marvellous, darling!' She flung her arms round his neck and hugged him. He stood, allowing himself to be held, then put an arm around her.

'I knew you could do it. I always knew.' She looked into his face; he was smiling.

'Daddy's going to be famous,' she said to me. 'I must tell Sadie and Ma.'

When we reached Sunnylands House, the trees were waving in the strong breeze. Ma, dressed in black, hair blowing across her face, was already on the doorstep. Head high, she smiled at me, and then looked down her nose at Mother.

'Isn't it great about the book?'

'Sadie, put on the kettle,' said Ma, leading the way into the kitchen.

At tea, Mother continued to be enthusiastic about the book. Sadie and Ma said little. Eventually Ma spoke.

'I always wanted him to go into the Church,' she said. 'He would have made a great preacher, wouldn't he, John?'

Pa did not reply. Mother looked at him.

'Aren't you pleased, Pa? Don't you want to read what your son wrote?'

The windows rattled with the wind.

'Cowboy stories is more his cup of tea,' said Ma. Pa stalked off to his shed.

'Well, Pa's cross,' said Sadie, 'and Ma's ashamed because the book's about labouring. My mother never forgave Tom for not going into the Church, and Pa doesn't have much time for books; he was always the sportsman. Even when he was working, he lived for sailing and swimming; then there was the rowing and the cycling.'

Mother looked perplexed; she had thought everyone would be pleased.

'Aren't you happy about the book?' she asked Sadie.

'Tom was never the same after the war. It ruined all our lives,' she said. 'Tom was meant for better than a labourer. And Sammy was never the same after that Japanese prisoner of war camp. Now he's working on the railways. As for my own troubles …'

Eventually *Clay Under Clover* was published by Gollancz and received a favourable review by Louis MacNeice in *The Observer*. My father was thrilled to read that he had been compared to one of his heroes, Pat MacGill, the Donegal writer-labourer and creator of Moleskin Joe.

IN THE SUMMERS I often went to stay at Sunnylands House. Ma and Pa still lived there just outside Carrickfergus. Natives of the town – she a dressmaker, he a solicitor's clerk – they had married in 1910. Soon afterwards he was offered Sunnylands House, rent free, in return for being the caretaker. This, together with his light duties as a rent collector, had given him ample time for sailing and cycling, two sports at which he excelled. At first they had the whole house to themselves and the children ran riot, often playing football in the ballroom. But when the wheelchair-bound Bates family came to share the house, they were given the front, which looked out over the lawn, while Ma, Pa and family moved to the back.

During the Troubles, Sir Dawson Bates, the Ulster politician, would sometimes go there for a break. He had overseen the signing of the Ulster Covenant, an anti-Home Rule pledge of which Pa, among 200,000 other men and women, had been a signatory on Ulster Day 1912. This covenant had been the stimulus for the setting up of the Ulster Volunteer Force of which Pa was a member, delivering messages on his racing bike by night.

Late at night Dawson Bates would slip in through a ground-floor window to his brother's part of the house and take a break from the vigorous politics of the day. Sometimes he would bring his bodyguard, Buck Alec, with him. This Protestant paramilitary killer was a well-known Belfast character who used to go out walking with his two pet lions, bought from a circus that once camped behind his house. It was rumoured that no cat or dog in the area was safe from being fed to Buck's lions.

Mr Bates, the politician's brother, paralysed from the waist down, was always in a wheelchair. Early each morning, his wife wheeled him outside. His legs were wrapped in a tartan blanket, and watercolour paints together with a milk bottle full of water were spread out before him on a tray. Hunched inside a heavy coat, he presided over the widest part of the avenue, his sharp eyes peering out from his horn-rimmed glasses. With trembling hands, Mr Bates painted until lunchtime, when he was wheeled back to the house. Then he was brought outdoors again until dusk. To the best of my knowledge, he only ever painted one thing: old sailing ships.

Sometimes during those summers I would watch him painting. He always did the ship first, then the sky above Sunnylands. Although the sky was different in every painting, the ship remained much the same.

One day I asked him why the sails were drooping and, as he put an unsteady touch to a cloud, he replied that there was no wind. But whenever I said anything about the Bates,

Ma and Pa were silent and it was some time before I found out why.

One of Pa's tasks as caretaker was to cut the big lawn at the front but since the grass grew about three feet high every summer, it had to be scythed. Pa's compact body could be seen bent to the work. When he straightened up, he would feel his back, ease the cap up on his head and gaze into the woods. Then he would reach into his back pocket for the sharpening stone, upend the scythe and, with deft strokes, sharpen the blade. My Aunt Sadie and I would take up pitch-forks and toss the fallen grass, this each day until it dried. Then everyone would gather it up and make pointed hay-stacks, turning the lawn into a hayfield.

In the evening, after tea, Pa would often clean his shotgun by the fire while Sadie played the piano. She and my mother had once played Dvorak duets together, but now Sadie played for me and as I sat on her knee we sang 'Paddy McGinty's Goat'. Pa liked her to play 'Home, Home on the Range' and he usually ended up humming along as he worked on the gun. When he was done, he peered up inside the barrel and snapped the gun shut.

I was always allowed to stay up late when I stayed with Ma and Pa. At the stroke of ten thirty, Pa would take the wire glasses off his nose, put aside the *Belfast News Letter* and lever himself slowly out of his armchair. When he had stretched, he reached high up to the mantelpiece above the range and felt for the metal key. Then, opening the glass face of the clock, he inserted the key and began winding with slow rhythmic strokes. Next, the glass globe was lifted from the oil lamp, the wick turned down and the flame blown out.

I didn't like going up the stairs at night. First you had to light the candle, cross the large black space at the foot of the stairs where the two funny-sounding pianos (they were harpsichords) stood, crumbling from woodworm. As I went up the steep staircase, the candle flame illuminated the bannister and its bars. Sometimes without warning, a mouse would run along one of the keyboards. It terrified me.

Even in summer, my room smelled of damp, but the bed, heavy with blankets, soon warmed up. Ma slept in a separate room, which had her own clock. It was solid brass and was wound with a hunting horn. It ticked quietly among a jungle of medicines. She was always taking to her bed where she supped large spoonfuls of Petrolagar, a thick white substance for her stomach; it came in tall bottles. As far as I could tell, she wasn't really ill but she seemed to like being in bed, where she would hold court with Sadie and Aunt Bith. In the mornings I would climb into her warm bed until she began tickling me, so I jumped out.

At home, my parents were always reading and when I asked questions they usually said 'Mm', absentmindedly turning another page. But at Sunnylands there were no books. Pa read only cowboy stories; he was unimpressed by what he called my father's 'book lernin'. Ma never read. One night, I opened Enid Blyton's *Island of Adventure*, and I couldn't put it down. When I told Ma I had read for two hours, she replied that reading wasn't good for you. I countered that my father read all the time. She went quiet for a while then spoke: 'I knew this man who started reading books, then he began writing poetry … Everyone said it was a sign of madness. He went mad the very next year.' So I learned not to mention reading to her but there was a topic she disliked even more.

At times I helped Pa in his shed. I liked it in there,

especially when it was raining. The drumming of the rain on the roof gave me a warm safe feeling and Pa would talk to me in what I called his 'indoor voice', as he showed me how to dismantle a shotgun. As he teased the oiled metal pieces apart and put them together again, I saw the tender care with which he handled the mechanism and soon I was dismantling and assembling the weapon myself. Pa was smiling, but as the blurry figure of Ma passed the wet window, he hastily put the gun back in the corner.

'I hope you haven't been teaching that boy about guns!' Ma snapped. Pa said nothing. I looked at the floor.

Breakfast was cooked on the range in the kitchen. It was a dull gleaming cast-iron stove with hot plates and an oven. Watched by Ma, Sadie would lift the frying pan and, opening the oven with a foot, remove a large log that was drying inside and dump it down in the range. Then, lifting an enormous black kettle, she would splash boiling water into a big china teapot before quickly emptying it out. She spooned in three lots of tea from the tin with a worn portrait of King George VI and the Queen. In splashed more hot water, steam rising to the high ceiling.

Each morning, logs were cut. My job was to wheel the wooden wheelbarrow. In it were a spade, a fork, an axe and the big crosscut saw. Whole days were spent cutting up fallen trees into logs for the big range in the kitchen. Pa took one end of the two-handled saw and I manned the other, but at the age of eight my presence was nominal. We would saw a slab off the thick trunk, and then he split it into logs. We worked in silence, the saw moving steadily back and forth through the trunk. I watched beetles scuttling about as the yellow sawdust showered on to the ground.

Around this time I had a dream: I went to the log we had been sawing, reached down underneath and pulled out a dark heavy object. I took it home and gave it to Pa, who put in on the mantelpiece and handed me sixpence. The next morning, still thinking of the dream, I went for a walk in the garden. As I stood looking at the log, I saw something underneath it. I reached down and pulled out a large axe head. I brought it back up to the house and handed it to Sadie, who looked at it in astonishment and called Pa. He came downstairs looking cross, but when he saw the axe head he stopped and took it in his hand. Weighing it, he shook his head and smiled. Sadie explained that twenty years earlier Pa had borrowed the axe from the Bates and had lost it. This had led to a huge row, after which they had hardly spoken. Pa gave me sixpence and put the axe head up on the mantelpiece.

Another unforgettable morning I rose early and found the pantry door, which was usually locked, open. I peeped inside. The morning light filtered through a coloured glass window at the far end. A bench ran the length of the narrow, whitewashed room which smelled of damp. When I pushed the door open further, I heard mice scurrying away. At first I could not focus but then I began to make out shapes. What was that long thing on the wall – could it be a gun? I stepped in and looked closer: it was a rifle. Turning to look behind me, I saw maybe half a dozen more, their polished wooden butts resting on the floor. Through the trigger guards ran a piece of thick wire securing them to the wall. It ended at a large padlock next to my knee. I fingered its oily keyhole, and my eyes, growing accustomed to the light, realized that there were more guns, mostly pistols, strewn on the bench. Suddenly I felt nervous and stood staring at the coloured window, unable to take in the enormity of it all. On a shelf, bullets spilled out of an overturned Oxo tin. My eyes fell on a wooden crate that had HAMBURG in black capitals on it.

Outside, a crow gave a single squawk as it crossed the yard. I came to my senses and, backing out of the room, left the door the way I had discovered it. I climbed the stairs quietly, undressed, put on pyjamas and slid back into the now cold bed. As I lay there, trying to warm up, a crow cawed in the tree outside my window. I wished I had never seen inside the pantry. When the warmth had returned to the bed, I fell asleep.

Later in the morning I woke and stared out the window at a blue sky, but as I looked out over the trees a cloud crossed the sun and I was in shadow. The guns. Deciding not to think about them, I dressed and started downstairs. When I passed the pantry door I hardly dared look, but with a quick glance, saw that it was shut.

I longed to ask someone about what I had discovered. I knew Pa had been involved in something called the 'Troubles' but I didn't understand what that was, except that some people got shot and that no one was supposed to mention it. At night I would lie awake thinking about the guns and in the mornings Ma would pronounce: 'That boy's not getting enough sleep!' I felt I had to speak to someone, but it couldn't be her.

A chance came one morning. Pa and I were sawing a tree trunk with the long crosscut saw. I saw the beads of sweat on his bald head – a sign that he would soon stop and mop his brow, and without speaking, he would grin, showing his teeth. But on this day, instead of resuming work, he paused a little longer than usual and I heard myself say: 'Granda, what are the Troubles?'

The question seemed to take him by surprise and the only sound was the crows rising noisily from the big tree. He was silent for a bit but then he told me that bad people had wanted to take Ulster away from the Ulster people. At times, he said, they used to stop the shooting in Belfast's York Street to allow the children get to school. I asked him if he had shot anyone. He was silent.

'God, the questions! The questions!' he said. 'I'll ask *you* a question then: when is a door not a door?'

I didn't know.

'When it's ajar!' he said, grinning. I couldn't see what jam jars had to do with doors or, for that matter with the Troubles.

'GO UP and light your Grandma's fire; she's taken one of her turns,' Sadie called to me late one winter's afternoon when I was over visiting. I got the sticks, picked up an old newspaper and climbed the stairs. This steep ascent always seemed to be like climbing into the sky. With Ma watching from bed, I raked out the grate, screwed the newspaper into balls and placed them on the dusty grille. Then I laid the sticks and last of all the logs. I put a lit match deep into the paper and sat back on the floor, watching the thin flames probe up into the sticks. When they caught fire, I could relax.

I rose and looked out of the bedroom window down to the deserted farmyard. In the middle was the rectangular dried-up duck pond, on one side the byre with no cows, on the other the stable with no horse. Above the stable was an empty dovecote – my favourite place when I wanted to get away from everything.

Ma took a large spoonful of her stomach medicine from the very tall bottle and swallowed it with satisfaction. I looked out at the fading winter light and saw a woman sailing across the yard in her hat and furs.

'Auntie Bith's coming!'

'Oh, she's early,' said Ma, fixing her hair in the hand mirror. The back door banged and presently Bith swept in, followed by Sadie. Ma was propped up in bed in her 'receiving visitors' mode.

'Ah Bith, how nice to see you,' said Ma and they kissed. I liked Bith – everyone said she was a howl. She always wore black, smelt of face powder and had a fox-fur draped around her neck. But I didn't like the dead fox's head, which rested on her left bosom. Its evil little glass eyes glittered.

Back beside the fire, I watched Ma's dark shape behind the wall of medicines on her bedside table, which was next to the window with a hole plugged by a wad of newspaper. Nobody would say how the hole had got there – at least no one would tell me, I thought, staring at the flames. Across the dark room Sadie, Bith and Ma were murmuring together in the firelight; occasionally there was laughter, usually provoked by Bith. Bored, I went over to look in the tray of a shaving mirror on the dressing table and my fingers touched something. In the dark it felt like a bullet. Rubbing it between my fingers, peering at it in the half-light, I felt the slippery brass and leaden point, all the while looking towards the women talking across the room. On a whim, I threw the small leaden object into the red part of the fire. Nothing happened. Dimly sensing that I should not stand in front of the fire, I moved aside. *Crack!*

'What's wrong? What is it?' Sadie called, astonished. My left hand was across one eye and I was screaming. She held up a candle; I could feel blood seeping between my fingers. As she prised away my fingers, I watched her frightened face with the other eye. The pain was terrible.

'The fire – it must have been something in the fire,' she said, helping me to press a towel to my bleeding eye. Ma, already out of bed, shouted down the dark stairs, 'John! John! Come quick.'

Pa appeared out of the darkness, his reading glasses up on his head.

'Look, John,' said Ma, holding up the candle so that he could see. The old man pushed his glasses on to his nose.

'Something from the fire,' Sadie said.

'There was a crack and he just put his hand to his eye,' said Ma, easing the towel from my bloody eye. Pa looked coldly at the wound; his face showed no reaction. He had seen wounds before, I thought.

'We've got to save the eye. I'll bring him on the bike.'

Ma held the candle high as we descended the dark staircase. Sadie had her arm round me. At the bottom Pa opened the pantry door, went inside and unhooked his racing bike from the ceiling. He slung it over his shoulder and steered me with his free hand out of the door and into the yard.

'Put your coat on,' Ma said and, when I was wrapped up, Pa put me on to the bar of his bike. I had not been on this before and as we sped off into the dark I was unprepared for how fast it would be. A racing bike, it had no lights, but my grandfather seemed unfazed by the darkness as we sped down the avenue and out on to the road. I held the towel to the eye with my left hand and gripped the handlebars with the other. A half-moon lit the surrounding fields; the only sound was the hum of the bike's hard tyres on the road. A fox barked. Pa had only recently given up racing, at the age of seventy-four. The dark hedges flew by until we swerved into the cottage hospital, narrowly missing a nurse going off duty.

She led us into Emergency, sat me up on a table, then gently peeled back the towel. I watched her expression as she looked at the eye, and saw her controlled face. She called loudly for Dr Hanna. By the time the doctor had inspected the wound, I could hear my father's motorbike outside. Pa went out to meet him and the two came in arguing.

'It's always guns with you isn't it?' my father said. 'One day you're teaching him to dismantle them and the next he's got a bullet in the eye. The Troubles are over this years now and you're still playing the cowboy, you oul' fool! Didn't you learn your lesson when –'

'Enough! He'll be all right – I saw that type of injury before. He still has the sight of the eye.'

'It must have been a bullet. I suppose they're still lying around the house.'

'He knows what bullets are, doesn't he?' he said turning to me. 'God knows, he's been out shooting with me often enough. Why would he be stupid enough to throw one on the fire?' My father said nothing.

The first school day after the accident I wore a pink patch over my left eye; cotton wool stuck out the sides. At break-time, while we sucked our ice-cold milk, the class inspected my patch. It had rows of tiny holes. I didn't like the colour or the cotton wool. There were still some cuts above the patch, which hinted at terrible damage to the eye itself.

The girls were very interested; I had never been so popular. 'Give us a look. Ah go on …' they chorused and eventually Sally Clausen – sulky Sally I called her – persuaded me and, in a corner of the playground, I lifted the pink patch. Her face turned from curiosity to horror: there was a gash where my eyebrow had been. After that, I saw her talking to her friends at the front of the class, who then stared back at me in pity.

At Halloween, Mother painted the patch black, which made me look more villainous. I went outside, and as I passed the kitchen window, I glanced at her; she was grinning at me through the geranium plant with a savage delight. I stared, shocked, at my reflection in the glass – I looked just like a pirate.

I WANTED very much to learn how to shoot and Pa had told me he would teach me. One windy day with nothing to do, I went looking for him and eventually found him in the shed, finishing a wooden gun butt with sandpaper.

'Could you teach me to shoot today?' I asked him without much hope. He half-turned from the bench.

'I'm busy now.'

'Please, Granda!'

'Later maybe. Your grandmother …' He tailed off worriedly but I saw that he was tempted.

'They're in having tea.'

'All right, only for a bit, mind. Go and get your gun.'

I had a small gun, which shot steel darts, and I slipped in the back door to get it. As I went through the scullery, I held the gun at my side, out of sight of the talking women. Out again, I broke open the small gun, slid in a green tufted dart and closed it. Raising the air gun to my right shoulder I sighted with my scarred left eye. Across the yard Pa was waiting by the shed door, which was covered in paint marks where brushes had been cleaned off. He pointed upwards.

'D'ye see that wee green bit there?' His voice bent in the wind but I nodded and without really seeing where he meant, raised the small gun to my shoulder and squeezed the trigger.

'That's miles off,' he shouted.

'Where's the mark, Granda?'

'Up there!' he said, pointing to the top of the door, but I was still uncertain.

'Where?'

Tears came to my eyes as I raised the gun again and fired. From his expression, I knew I had missed. Unknown to both of us my mother had just come into the yard.

'What do you think you're doing – teaching him to shoot?' she shouted over the wind, arms rigid at her sides. Ma came out and stood, a dark figure, in the doorway.

'Guns, guns – it's always guns, isn't it, John?'

Pa looked defeated by the women and would not meet my eye. Something had changed between us: I was not a good shot.

The following weekend, back home at Trooperslane, Father, Mother and I came in from walking the dogs.

'Can I help you off with your boots?' I asked.

'What?' my father said, looking surprised. Then he started laughing. I went red.

'But I always did it for Granda!'

'I'm not an old man. You only pull off boots for old men!' he said, still laughing. I had not realized that Pa was old.

While my mother was preparing dinner in the kitchen and Father was absorbed in his newspaper, I took out my cowboy gun and pointed it at the wall of paper. My father unexpectedly lowered it to find himself looking down the muzzle of the black gun. He went white, his lips parted and the paper slipped from his hands. He looked terrified. With a dry mouth that softened his voice to a near croak, he said: 'Don't ever, *ever* point a gun at me again!' and I knew I never would, for in that moment I sensed that my father knew something about guns – something very bad. Mother, overhearing the conversation, came in from the kitchen and told him about the shooting lesson.

'Guns!' he said to me in disgust. 'That'll learn you!'

Although in later years during military service I was trained to use rifle and machine gun, I never came to like guns or like them near me.

ALTHOUGH, as a nine year old I knew Pa was old, I had only just come to realize this, and on my next visit to Sunnylands I learned he was vulnerable too. I had crossed the farmyard to the byre and climbed the broken ladder, which led up to the dovecote above the stable. Because I was light, I could climb the ladder without breaking it further. I liked to go there and sit among the empty perches and nest boxes. Mostly I played with a plastic word puzzle or watched what was going on in the stable through cracks in the floor below where Dash, the Irish red setter, slept on hay laid on the cobbled floor. I soon discovered that I could hear anyone below talking while they fed him.

One day my mother came in with Sadie, they seemed to be arguing.

'Well, Ross says he saw guns in the pantry,' my mother was saying. 'What on earth was Pa up to in the Troubles?'

'He won't say, but Bith says all the UVF were involved in the Larne guns. It was before my time – I was only a baby.'

Bith had told her that Pa had been involved in running guns into Larne. Thousands of guns and millions of bullets had been landed at the port. I listened astonished as Sadie said that Bith had actually been there, in Larne staying with her aunt. She had only been a girl at the time but she and her cousins had all spent the night playing in the streets. They had even sneaked down to the port in the drizzling rain to watch the arms being unloaded by the light from all the car headlights but they were chased back home by UVF men. In the town itself, Bith said, all the lights were on and mothers and their children were out in the streets until dawn when the last of the arms left town. Now I knew that my grand-father had been a soldier after all and I began to see him with new eyes – as a hero.

Somehow Pa found out I had been in the dovecote and decided to investigate, so I led him along the eaves to the place where I would sit.

'You'd want to be careful here,' he said, 'the floor's not safe.'

Just then there was a crack and he went straight down through the floor. At the last minute he spread his arms and saved himself from falling to the cobbles below. Our eyes met – he looked afraid.

'Don't tell your grandmother,' he said as he took my arm, struggled out of the hole and dragged himself to the floor near the wall.

The next day when I was up in the dovecote I heard the sound of voices. I peeped down through the hole: Ma and Mother were below in the stable feeding Dash. They were talking about the hole in the ceiling.

'It looks like someone fell through. Remember when Sadie fell through the kitchen ceiling?' said Ma laughing. I had been there too when, without warning, Sadie's leg had come through in a shower of plaster.

'The whole place is falling down,' said Ma. 'It'll not be here long – and neither will we.'

THE END of Sunnylands, when it did come, was signalled by a simple event. One morning the water in the scullery suddenly stopped coming out of the tap. Sadie and I crossed the fields to investigate and were astonished to find a huge hole, dug deep with steep sides. We stood on the edge and looked far down at a huge lake of dirty water. In the middle, with water half up its cab, was an excavator. The driver was up on the roof.

'We've no water because of you,' Sadie called to him.

'Will you call for some help and get me out of here? I'm stranded!' shouted the driver, who was surrounded by water.

It turned out that Sunnylands had finally been sold. It was to become the Sunnylands housing estate in whose local school Sadie was later to teach. After thirty years of living in the old house, Ma and Pa were given three months' notice to leave. Since the house in Trooperslane belonged to them, they would move in there and we would have to find a new home.

MY FRIEND MARK and I were playing in the river at the bottom of our garden at Trooperslane. We had spent the morning sitting up on our log in the small field between our house and the station, writing down the numbers of the steam engines that stopped at Trooperslane. The only engine with no number came droning heavily into the station – a diesel we called The Harlandic.

'We have to leave this house, my Daddy says,' I shouted over the noise.

'What?' Mark shouted.

'My Granny and Granda and Aunt Sadie are coming to live in our house.'

'But where will you live?'

'I don't know. I think by the sea.'

'Where on earth have you got to?' my mother called.

I came out from the small field behind the garden hedge. There she stood, pregnant on the bridge.

'You have to go now – your father's waiting!'

The motorbike engine fired and, leaving Mark in the field, I ran out and jumped into the sidecar. We were on our way to Sunnylands for the last time.

Once there, he cut the engine and I ran over to the iron gate leading to the garden. He joined me, resting his arms on top of the gate and gazing out over his childhood fields. Before us was a vast hilly mudscape; two excavators stood idle in the distance. As we watched, a bright yellow earth-moving vehicle with huge tyres sped by. My father was silent. I noticed a rabbit crouching in the hedge and pointed, but my father turned away and, without speaking, we went up to the house.

In the warm kitchen the mood was sombre, the only sound an occasional log slipping in the range.

'I hear Millie's mother is going to help you buy a house,' Ma said to my father.

'Yes, we're going to see somewhere on the beach.'

'Whereabouts is that?' Pa asked as Ma got up to light the oil lamp.

'Eden, below the railway there –'

'Mind out, Ma!' Father called as the glass globe slipped out of her fingers and skittered across the table. It smashed on the floor.

'WE'RE GOING to see the new house today,' my father said one Saturday morning as we crunched our burnt toast. Mother was still in hospital having the baby; home was quiet without her. I asked how we would get there for I knew the motorbike had broken down.

'We'll take the train.'

'But what about the dogs?'

'Natasha and Sassy can come on the train with us.'

We walked down the path and crossed the wooden bridge. It had been raining heavily in the night and the swollen river roared under our feet.

We didn't take the platform from which Father used to go to work in Belfast as we were going in the other direction, to Carrickfergus.

'One and a half returns to Eden please. Oh, and tickets for the dogs,' my father said.

'Eden? I don't think the next one stops there. Most of the trains don't,' said the portly stationmaster who was standing nearby.

'I checked the timetable, Andy.'

The man went over to a large black and white timetable on the wall, avoiding the borzoi and labrador who were sniffing at the skirting board.

'Oh, right enough, it does!' he said, drawing his finger along the straight black lines of the poster-size timetable.

'It's a stormy spot – the station fell in the sea last year,' the stationmaster added, looking out at a sun shower. We all gazed at the rainbow against the dark green of Knockagh hill. In the waiting room the dead man's motorbike was still gathering dust. Running late for work one morning, Mr Hannah, our cleaning woman's husband, who used to wave to me in the mornings, had been killed trying to get around the closing gates at the level crossing. The train had crushed him against the edge of the platform.

My father stared at the dust-covered motorbike, saying nothing, but then he rarely spoke. I peered into his lean, bearded face, looking for a sign of his mood, for he often flew off the handle without warning. I started to ask about the house at Eden, but my voice was drowned by the noise of the train arriving. We went on to the platform and saw the steam engine coming towards us; it was back to front today, pulling the carriages. The black locomotive came to rest with a low screech. Doors began opening and slamming shut.

'Carrick, Larne …' the guard shouted, 'Stopping at Eden and Kilroot,' he added as we got the dogs up into the coach. Soon we were speeding through the countryside while I watched the shadow of the engine's smoke on the fields scattered with black and white bullocks. Natasha was curled up on the floor, head on paws. Sassy sat with her head by my knee.

'You know we don't have much money, don't you?' my father asked, looking bleak. 'This house is smaller,' he said. But it's by the sea.'

I liked the sea and had been fishing once on Carrick Quay with my Uncle Sammy and Aunt Joan when they had come over from England. They had gone into Bell's shop and bought the two green fishing lines I had been gazing at for months. And they had cost half a crown each! It had been a wild, blowy day at the end of the harbour and when my aunt caught a flatfish, she screamed with delight and fear.

As we were drawing into Carrickfergus station, I looked up at the sky through the thicket of corks pegged to the telephone wires. I asked Father what the corks were for and he told me they were to stop homing pigeons hitting them and hurting themselves.

'Will Mummy be coming home soon?'

'When the baby comes.' We watched the passengers disappearing down the dark steps into the town. A mournful-looking porter was taking tickets at the gate.

'He was one of the stay-at-homes,' said my father. 'He didn't want to fight Hitler.'

In the quiet of the morning, strong puffs from the engine drew us out of the dark station and into sunshine. Soon the train went into a tunnel. Then we burst into the light again.

'We need air in here,' Father said, lowering the window. I stood up and put my head out, enjoying the wind and looking down at the passing shore.

'It's nearly our stop,' he said, getting to his feet.

I turned, surprised.

'But there's nothing here!'

'Over there!' My father pointed to the landward side of the train and I saw a scattered collection of coloured wooden bungalows. Most of them were dark green, one or two were blue, but one stood out: bright yellow with red window frames. The train stopped at a platform fashioned from railway sleepers and cinders. On a weather-beaten board I could just make out the name EDEN HALT.

My father and I, Natasha and Sassy stood gazing over the railway lines at the sea. On the still, shining water the silhouettes of sea birds stood out against the bright water, some motionless, some flying along the surface. We crunched along the railway cinder path, past the yellow bungalow. I thought I saw a curtain move. Across the railway lines, we stopped to read a concrete notice: 'Beware of trains – Stop, Look, Listen.'

Father went through the turnstile gate first, and then we stepped down towards the shore. He was first across the bridge and, as I watched, the boards flexed under his weight. Then it was my turn. I looked down at the fast-flowing water and followed the river with my eye to where it fanned out in silver across the flat shore to meet the sea.

We walked along a stony path above the shore, past a row of bungalows. The first one was grey and white; the next one was small and green with carefully trimmed hedges. The path was breached in places; I looked at the waves breaking farther out at the ebb tide.

'Does no one live here?' I asked, looking at the blank windows. My father strode on until we reached a gap in the houses. An express train hurtled past the space. As it faded into the distance, the silence was dense.

'That's it, there,' said father, letting the dogs free of the leash and pointing to a freshly painted green bungalow with white window frames. At the front was a glass porch; a single red geranium inside. On the left side were the remains of a boat and on the right a pile of wood. All was enclosed by a low, tarred, paling fence. The front gate gave on to a narrow cement path with a small lawn on either side. Round the corner of the bungalow, we stood staring at a rowing boat. I looked towards the boards of the house: it wasn't even made of bricks! Seeing the expression on my face, Father hurried me to the back door and opened the padlock.

'Go on in. I'm off down the beach. I'll be back shortly.' He put Mother's binoculars round my neck.

I walked in through a narrow kitchen to the front room, my footsteps echoing in the empty wooden house. The boards of the walls were a faded pale green; the ceiling had two fly-stickers, covered with long-dead casualties. There were two doors. I opened the first: the room was empty except for a chamber pot and a birdcage. Then I opened the second, and saw a wire bed frame with no mattress. Under it was a black shoe. Back in the front room, I caught the scent of geraniums. As I walked into the porch, with its bright windows, I lifted the leather-covered binoculars round my neck; polished brass gleamed where the leather had worn through. One eyepiece was broken and felt slightly jagged to the eye, but they had a lived-in feel. With elbows on the high window ledge beside the single geranium, I lowered myself to the eyepieces. Where were the dogs? I adjusted the focus on three crooked wooden stakes set in the shingle below the house. There was a strong breeze now: the sun was shining down on wet sand, which reflected the moving clouds. I examined a sloping stone sea wall. I could see we were in a small bay.

Out on the sand a man and a boy were flying a kite; a woman stood nearby. Then there was a gust of wind and the kite broke free. It rose rapidly and was soon careering wildly until it became a red fleck and then a dot. I was suddenly uneasy, but then a shower began to drum loudly on the roof and I felt warm and safe: it was just like Pa's shed. Natasha and Sassy scrambled through the back door, their claws clacking on the linoleum and, before I could stop them, they shook the rain off vigorously and I jumped back, laughing.

When they settled, I put my hand on Sassy's wet head and stroked her gently, the way my mother did to me when I came home from school. She would tell me about the birds she had seen that day: I liked that. Once I had seen a goldfinch at our bird table and sometimes a fat wood pigeon would come, crowding out the other birds.

As the pregnancy progressed, Mother was quieter and I would put my ear to her tummy to listen for the baby, wondering what I was supposed to hear. Then one day the doctor had come and serious faces had spoken about something called 'complications'. The ambulance arrived and took her to hospital. Home was strange without her. Father didn't say much and never answered my questions.

When I took up the binoculars again, I started looking through them the wrong way. As I pointed them at the sea wall, everything was tiny and far away. Just at that moment a small figure came round the corner of the sea wall. Putting the glasses back the right way, I looked through them again and jumped at the hugeness of Father, striding towards me.

'We're about done here. Let's go home,' he said. As we locked up and left, dusk was falling and I looked back at the house. It wasn't a real house but inside it was like Pa's shed.

As we reached the Halt, the lamps were being cleaned and lit by a railway worker. One already cast its yellow light. My father talked quietly with the man while I brought the dogs into the tin hut. It smelt. Standing there were two boys in kilts – identical twins. I stared. Sassy let them pat her, Natasha stood aloof. Presently the black engine steamed up to the Halt, its huge steel wheels glistening with oil in the darkness.

'No dogs on the train,' the guard said, silhouetted against the van's light.

'The other guard let us on,' my father said.

'Well, it's against the rules. You can walk, or ride home on the dog's back.' He laughed.

'Well you haven't changed anyway, Billy McCallion.' The guard stopped and peered closely at my father.

'My God, Tom, it's you. Do you mind we used to sit together in school?'

'Well, are you going to leave us standing here, Billy?'

'Let them on Billy, for God's sake,' said a big woman who had stuck her head out of her compartment window.

'No, no, get on, get on, Tom. Is that your boy there?' the guard said, pointing to me.

Inside, the woman started petting Sassy. Beside her was a large man in gumboots.

'What class of a dog is that?' he said, squinting at Natasha.

'That's a Russian wolfhound — a borzoi,' said my father proudly.

'Tom, you tell Pa you met Dick — Deadeye. Tell him I was askin' for him,' he said when he got off at Carrickfergus. It wasn't until we ourselves left the train at Trooperslane that I remembered my mother was in hospital.

OUR MOVE from the suburbs to a beach shack occured when I was nine and coincided with the birth of my brother, Joss. When my parents came home in a taxi with the new baby, Father could scarcely contain himself from taking Mother upstairs to the landing. There, he pointed out the window and down into the garden where the wooden frame of a canoe lay upside down on trestles. During her absence, he had built it from scratch. I listened as he retold the story about how Eskimos would flip over their canoes so that they could harpoon fish, then flip them right side up again.

'We'll have a new start, a whole new life at the beach!' he said.

Mother was silent and looked doubtful. I only knew that I didn't want to leave my friend Mark.

The baby was to be christened Joscelyne after a friend of my parents in the RAF, but on his way to have the silver christening mug engraved, Father forgot the spelling and he ended up being called Jocelyn. In later years it was shortened to Joss and so the two of us were to have rhyming names: Ross and Joss.

One September morning, we moved house. No one came out to say goodbye, but I saw Mark watching from his garden, while three carters helped load up to begin the journey to Kilroot beach below Eden.

My bearded father, wearing a beret, sat on top of the leading cart. It was drawn by a white horse borrowed from the milkman, who, dressed as King William, would ride it at the head of the Twelfth of July parade into Carrick. The second cart was piled with all Father's books. On top of the books was the canoe. Up on the last cart, which held all the furniture, my mother and I sat with the baby.

After an hour the horses and carts turned off the main road by Eden Orange Hall and we started down a lane. The whole convoy rattled and creaked its way along, scraping the hedges all the way downhill to Loughside farm, where we could see the sea glittering through the tree trunks.

Across the railway lines, the horses were halted at the wooden bungalow and their nosebags put on. As they munched away, the carters, helped by Father, deposited furniture and books on the slanting shingle between house and beach. Mother sat on a rock with the weeks-old baby on her knee.

When the rattling of harness and bumping of empty carts had died away, we stood on the shingle incline watching the sea birds. They were feeding in groups amongst the seaweed, smaller birds taking off in singles and pairs to land a few feet away. Along the shore in the shallows some cattle stood knee-deep in water.

During a pause and without warning my mother thrust the baby into Father's arms and before he could protest she opened the piano which was on the shingle and began to play. It was a piece of ragtime and the notes carried across the small bay and echoed off the sea wall. The baby started to cry and she took it again. Just then, a tall white-haired man in dungarees came along the path and offered to help carry our things inside. We learned he was Willie Smith and he considered himself to be in charge of the bungalows.

On my way in and out I passed through the kitchen and each time I was awestruck by the sight of the giant Victorian iron bath. At first, the house had echoed with every step, but since it was filled with furniture there was a flatter sound to our footsteps. After two hours of carrying, we were all hungry. Willie and Father finally edged a wardrobe sideways through the kitchen and there was only the piano left outside. Mrs Smith brought tea which we had out on the shingle.

It was getting cold, so Father threw a tarpaulin over the piano and we went inside. Willie said he would look in next day. In the middle of the floor of the front room Mother started the Primus and we had beans on toast, the toast made by scorching it on the stove. Afterwards, Father pulled off some pieces of the old boat outside, and as the day faded, the stove began to blaze. I watched the flames through little square mica windows in the stove front. When it became too hot, I went outside to look at the evening high tide. As I stared out in the twilight, I saw a dark shape floating: it was triangular, like a tilted box. Then it struck me: it was the piano! Too afraid to tell anyone I went back inside.

As night fell on our first night in the bungalow we sat around the stove, listening to Jimmy Shand and his Band on the wireless. It was quite warm and Joss was asleep; the three of us were tired and dreamy.

A thumping at the front window jolted us awake, Father got up and opened it. There was a cry like that of a wounded bear and the *Belfast Telegraph* was thrust into his hand. It was the paper man, Mr Coles, who had a cleft palate. He vanished into the night and, after closing the window, my father stood there with the paper and a bewildered look on his face.

Mother explained that she had ordered the papers from Coles' shop in the village and that the wife was from Dublin. I noticed the interest in her voice and asked where it was. My parents looked at each other.

'It's in Éire – the Free State,' my father said.

ON THE FIRST MORNING, a Saturday, I was wakened by the sound of waves crashing on the beach and saw light from a small square window above my bed; I lay staring up at it. A cock crowed. Next door was my parents' bedroom from which you could see the sea, mine looked out on to a tall hedge. Joss was sleeping in a wooden cot in a small room next to mine.

I got out of bed and grasped the tiny brass door handle: the door itself was flimsy and felt strange, not like the old house. In my pyjamas, I went out and, squeezing past the tallboy, turned into the long thin kitchen. On my way to the back door, I stopped again to marvel at the huge cast-iron bath with its single giant tap.

Once I got outside I looked up at the black rainwater barrel, then at a slow goods train, its wheels moving at eye level behind the back hedge. It suddenly stopped and the trucks bumped into each other. In the brief silence I could hear the waves before the trucks jolted again and the train moved on.

Back inside the house, my bare feet padded through the silent sitting room with its faded pale green walls. Boxes of books were everywhere and I weaved between them to the porch which had tall, oblong panes all around. I gazed out at the vastness of the beach. The binoculars were still lying on the sill. I looked at the homely, leather-covered glasses. I pointed them out at the huge expanse of sand exposed by the ebb tide. Here and there were dark stretches of rock and seaweed. To the west across the weeded sand lay the castle, to the east a sloping sea wall curled out, guarding the small bay.

I sat down on a wooden chair. After a creaking of bed-springs, Mother came in wearing her dressing gown.

'Morning, darling.' She took a chair.

'Isn't it lovely here? Your father's gone to work.' She leaned back to let the sun light up her face.

After breakfast I went outside. The porch at the front had a pointed roof and in the triangle above the windows was a painted placard with The Bungalow written in yellow letters on a green background. I looked down the walls of the house: it was up on concrete blocks. I got down on my knees and looked underneath but could see only the gap of daylight on the other side. I started crawling under; I could just fit and, peering into the dark, crawled farther. Then I saw it: in the centre under the house was a large black hole. I felt afraid and I wondered what was at the bottom or if it even had one. I backed out quickly. Mother knocked on the steamy kitchen window, so I went round to the back door. Joss was already in the pram and, crossing the railway line, we headed for the lane to the village.

As we closed the iron gate we entered the farmyard where a big man, beret pulled down over his ears, was standing in gumboots barring our way. Mother had told me she had heard that when Don was a boy he had been sitting on his mother's knee at the piano when someone had come in wearing a Halloween mask. He had apparently gone mad on the spot and never recovered. Mother said he was harmless, but as we passed through the farmyard I wasn't so sure. There Don stood, head down, talking to the ground. He wandered across, eyes fixed on me.

'Wheryougoin now?' he said. I froze.

'Wheryougoin? Wheryougoin?'

'We're going up to the village, Don,' my mother said loudly and clearly in her English voice. The big man seemed satisfied and moved away. As we walked up the lane, I looked back and saw him pick up two buckets of water and carry them off.

Mother and I had to push the pram through mud and puddles. As we came round a sharp bend in the lane, we heard the sound of a pipe band starting up in the distance. First two drum rolls, then the ragged bagpipes came together in 'Cock o' the North', but stopped. A single piper briefly broke into a few bars of 'The Sash My Father Wore'. Then all was quiet. We came within sight of the main road and glimpsed the pipers' tartan. As we drew close, I could see bandsmen smoking. The bass drum was inscribed STAR OF EDEN PIPE BAND.

I pushed Coles' shop door to let Mother wheel in the pram; there was a loud ping from the bell. Mrs Coles, a dark, stout woman, was leaning over the counter. Mother asked for twenty Gallagher's Blues.

'Did you get the paper?' the shopkeeper asked brusquely.

'Yes, thank you, Mrs Coles. Could we have the *Manchester*

Guardian every day and *The Observer* on Sunday? Oh, and some sweets. Cadbury's Milk, please.'

'Have you your coupons?' She held up a pair of nail scissors tied to the counter with a string. Mother produced the Ration Book, a square was snipped out and handed back.

We crossed the street to the grocers – Dan Rea, the grocer, was dumpy, bald on top with grey fringes left at the sides. He delivered groceries to the bungalows in the boot of his car. We stood in the dark barn-like shop. Sacks of peas, lentils and potatoes rested on the floor. Mother asked for half a pound of cheese. The grocer heaved a large cheese on to a slab. Then he lifted a length of wire, and holding the wooden peg on the end, stretched it, and drew it evenly down through the cheese, making a beautiful clean cut with sharp, straight edges.

Last of all we visited Miss Reid in the Post Office. She was grey-haired with steel-rimmed glasses and an earnest manner. Mother bought stamps for the letters she wrote to her family in England. Outside was the red pillar box and a phone booth. At that time only the rich had phones in their homes; everyone else had to use this phone box. To call the doctor, Mother had to walk a mile up the lane and then perhaps stand waiting in the Post Office for her turn.

That lunchtime when my father got home, he went to change out of his work clothes. Mother and I sat down at the table among boxes for tea and she asked about the piano.

'Tom!' she shouted, 'where's the piano?'

Father emerged, pulling on his trousers.

'Wasn't it out on the beach?' He rushed to the window. 'Oh Christ, we must have left it out. We left it well up. It should still be there.'

We all three of us went outside.

'Where could it have gone?' my father asked. 'It was standing just there.' He pointed to a spot beside three stakes in a
sandy part of the shingle. 'Was the tide out a long way this
morning?' he said to me and I told him it had been miles out.
'Oh God, it must have been a spring tide last night. It came
right up.'

He looked at my mother. Tears came to her eyes and
mopping them with the end of her apron, she turned and
went back inside. After a few minutes I followed, to find her
doing the washing up. Tears were streaming down her cheeks
into the suds.

'I knew we shouldn't have come here,' she said, then turned
to look at me. 'That piano was everything to me and your
father doesn't care. I know he doesn't. It was from Prague.
Dvorak's city – he died there.'

IT WAS some time before we learned to understand Mr Coles.
He delivered the newspapers in all weathers. On stormy nights
the rain poured off his sou'wester and oilskins as we exchanged
a few unintelligible words through the open window. Milk
was delivered from a crate in the back of a saloon car and
Ormeau Joe, who was a bit simple, drove the bread van.

Only a handful of people stayed there the whole year
round, one of whom was the patriarch of the small bay, Willie
Smith. He was a retired carpenter and involved himself in
every aspect of beach life and was faintly resented by the
other residents. Our next-door neighbours, Jack and Lily
Evans, were all-year-round residents. Jack drove a lorry and
each morning when he left for work, Lily spent a while
building and rebuilding their breakwater with rocks. Their

garden and bungalow were the best shielded from the winter seas that threatened to engulf the small gardens.

There were fifteen bungalows as well as a railway carriage, where Jackie lived. A small wizened man with a noisy Excelsior two-stroke motorbike, he usually had a rifle slung over his shoulder as he rode the lanes up to the main road. His wife, Violet, was a big woman who wore floral dresses and was forever knitting. Farther up the beach was Sammy Calderwood, a carpenter from the shipyard, Fred, an odd-job man, Mr Clarke, a fitter, and finally Mr Green, who had geometrical hedges at which he snipped carefully. He was gardener for Miss Higgins, whose mansion and estate, Rosganna, dominated the east of our small bay.

This estate was bounded on the railway side by a tall stone wall and on the seaward side by a downward-sloping sea wall. Connecting the two was a high wooden fence with a single wicket gate at which I often stood staring deep into a dark quiet wood. The edifice of Rosganna rose up above tall trees; I almost never saw anyone there. The seagulls never went there either, ignoring its green lawns stretching to the sea wall. Only crows flapped their way across the faded yellow big house that faced outwards to the wider lough. Everyone knew Miss Higgins lived there in retirement, but few had ever seen her and then only a glimpse, as her Austin Princess swept out the gates, over the railway crossing and away.

Often, walking the length of the row of bungalows, I would end up on the cinder path gazing up the high, weathered wooden paling at the slender trees bent in a gale, crows clinging to their black, untidy lumps of nests in the top branches. Without warning they would rise, cawing, then resettle moments later.

The railway cinder path went in a dead straight line towards the horizon, where on a clear day you could see Scotland. Sometimes I walked past Miss Higgins' big gates and on to the deserted Victorian railway station at Kilroot, with its empty signal box and weeds on the windowsills and roofs. From the platform I could look down onto where a field jutted out to sea, its cattle spilling on to the beach. When the tide was out, they would wander along the shore to the bungalows and usually ended up munching the hedges and leaving cow-crap everywhere.

At other times I went to the sea end of the paling fence and round the corner called The Point. If the tide was in, I would walk along the top of the sea wall and look across the grazing sheep to the empty windows of the big house. One day I saw the lady of the house walking among the sheep quite close to where I was standing at the top of the sea wall, but she did not notice me.

There were, we discovered, two lanes up to Eden village from the beach. The nearest to us, just over the railway, was the Orange Hall Lane. The biggest problem for me using that lane was that it was barred by Don. I had learned that although the madman was mostly harmless, there were times when he did lose control. Once some boys had thrown stones at him and provoked him. Then they had to run for their lives but Don cornered them and lashed them about the legs with his belt. Afterwards he went home and attacked his mother who had him committed to Purdysburn mental asylum again.

On the days when I could not face Don, I took the other lane. To get there I walked along the path in front of the bungalows and crossed the three-plank bridge over the river from where I could see the smoke from a makeshift house.

Alan, an old tramp, had built himself a house from driftwood and cement high up on the beach. Smoke always came from a rusty stovepipe poking out the top. He collected driftwood that was piled high behind his improvised house. Outside was a notice, painted roughly on a piece of rusty tin: 'Beware of the dog – Survivors prosecuted'. Whenever I walked past, a dog started barking inside and Alan would emerge wearing an old hat, his coat tied in the middle with binder twine. Bessie, his black and white collie, would crouch, barking at you until he hauled her inside. They said Alan lived off bread and sugar sandwiches that he washed down with strong tea.

Above the shore, through the wooden gate, was the railway line and primitive station – Eden Halt – whose structure jutted out over the sea wall. Inside, through the cracks in the floor of railway sleepers, you could hear and glimpse the waves on the sea wall below.

After crossing the railway lines, you passed between a yellow and a green bungalow, then followed the rising lane as it twisted among different-coloured dwellings. At a bend in the lane you passed Lockhart's shop, in the back of which Jim and his sister Annie lived. The cottage was as quiet as the grave and often had a huge puddle outside. Inside, you were in a small space four feet square with the counter on the left. It was very dark because it had no electricity. After about a minute's wait, Jim's pale face would appear in the dusk behind the counter. More like a ghost than a man, sometimes he would be holding a black Bible, his finger keeping his place. Jim had a more pagan side, for every morning, he would go down to the railway gate to salute the rising sun. On summer evenings he would stand staring at the setting sun. He wore a collarless shirt with the collar stud keeping it closed. If you passed him or his sister in the lane, their pale expressionless faces gave little away and, apart from a religious lamp and flame, their low, whitewashed cottage on the bend in the lane never showed signs of life.

One day I had gone to the shop for potatoes and Jim brought me across the lane to a pair of tall wooden doors. Producing a bundle of keys, he undid a large padlock. As he unlocked the door, I stared at the rotten holes at the base, thinking I could easily have crawled underneath. Inside were sacks of potatoes and rusty weighing scales. Jim took the scoop from the scales and asked me if I wanted a stone. I nodded and he shook potatoes from a sack into the scoop and put it on the scales. He changed the iron weights and the potatoes went up, then he began to throw single potatoes in to make the scales balance. I held out an old shopping bag and, head down, he poured them into it.

'The Lord giveth and the Lord taketh away,' he intoned as they rattled into the bag.

Farther up the lane, at Big Alec Lockhart's house, tumbler pigeons were somersaulting in the air. They were tan and white and on good days as they tumbled, their white under-feathers flashed in the sun. Some birds would strut on the loft roof while others took off across the fields. Their beauty was new to me.

SUMMER WAS nearly over and most of the bungalows were empty, as their owners returned to Belfast. This meant that there were only a few neighbours remaining with us as we entered into our first winter on the beach.

One night I lay awake, listening to the gale tearing at the boards of the wooden house. I was playing with the idea that the whole bungalow would lift off, be blown across the railway and dumped in the fields. Between the buffets of wind, I heard the thunder of the waves on the shore and, listening for them, fell asleep.

I woke a little later. The storm was still raging and the moonlight streamed through my small window. Something told me to get out of bed and, going into the front room, I was surprised to see my mother holding the big metal alarm clock and peering out at the sea, which seemed to be everywhere. Just then a cloud covered the moon and white waves could be seen in the dark, close up to our garden fence.

I asked her what the clock was for and she told me she was waiting for high tide.

'With your father away, I'll not relax till the sea goes down.'

We stood there together for some time until the clouds moved away from the moon and the garden was lit up. Mother pointed out at our small lawn; the grass square was rising and falling, heaving like a breathing chest in the moonlight. I was amazed. She said the tide was in the drains and that the waste pipe under the grass must be broken.

Suddenly she opened the front door, ran out and stood on the heaving hump. I grinned in the dark as she rose and fell, laughing up at the sky, then I ran out and joined her. Holding hands, rising and falling, we laughed until it grew cold and went inside. She made hot pea soup, which we sipped from mugs. Then, as the tide had fallen a bit, we went back to bed.

In the morning, the clanking of the goods train behind the house woke me. I got up and looked out of the front window: most of the road had disappeared and our fence lay on its side, diagonal to the house. Seaweed was piled up to the doorstep.

The breakfast toast was burnt; she always made it like that. I liked it — the black bits with the marmalade. Afterwards I struggled into my coat and Mother buttoned it up and handed me my leather schoolbag. Out the back door I gazed up at the chequered Antrim hills and, rounding the corner of the house, felt the breeze on my cheeks.

The beach was peaceful and still, destruction was everywhere. Even the gulls seemed a bit dazed. Huge banks of weed covered the foreshore with scattered pieces of wood. The tide was far out now but angry waves thundered silently in the distance. The sky was dark and the distant sea brown when suddenly the sun broke through and the waves were bathed in a shaft of intense light. I picked my way along the remains of the road. It was difficult climbing over slippery rocks with a heavy schoolbag, but jumping from rock to rock, I made good progress. Shoes squelching, I crossed the railway line and joined the lane up to the village.

I walked through the smoky village of Eden, whose only street was the main road. A horse and orange cart was jingling towards me. As I walked up the village, the sounds of the cart receded behind me. I looked back, thinking of the move from Trooperslane. I felt we had lived in a real house then, its river in the garden had a kind of musical tinkle, not like the roar of the waves at night. I thought of my friend Mark. Why did we have to leave? I recalled the afternoon our belongings were deposited on that beach. As the carts jolted away along the path above the shore, we had stood on the shingle – four including baby Joss, among our boxes and furniture. The canaries Pa had given us were fighting in their cage and I had put my coat over it to quieten them.

The Primary School was a low white building in the middle of the village. I was late. A woman with a red face and frizzy hair came out of a classroom door.

'Ross Skelton?'

'Yes, Miss.'

'Miss Sloan is sick. I'm your teacher today: Miss Young!' She brought me into the classroom.

'Now, children, I want you to welcome the new boy.' She looked around for a space: there was only one at a double desk. She took my coat. I sat down and looked at my neighbour: a boy with dirty uneven teeth. He looked at me without curiosity.

'Now, children – we'll begin with the hymn: "Jesus Loves Me".' They began singing:

> *Jesus loves me, this I know*
> *For the Bible tells me so ...*

The boy beside me was playing with something in his hands under the desk.

'All together now,' called the teacher as we came into the chorus.

> *Yes, Jesus loves me*
> *Yes, Jesus loves me,*

It was a sliver of glass. The boy pointed it towards me. He jabbed at me and I jumped back in alarm. Miss Young's bulging eyes were on me as she conducted the hymn, singing loudly.

> *Yes, Jesus loves me*
> *The Bible tells me so ...*

As the song continued, the boy kept jabbing the glass towards me. I looked into his eyes – they were laughing! He jabbed again; now he was grinning. I was alarmed and calmed at the same time for it was almost as if he wanted to play with me.

At break-time I couldn't get away from my tormentor, Eddie Creighton, who seemed to have adopted me. The two of us stood outside, hands numb, silently sucking ice-cold milk through straws out of glass bottles. Dark green hills could be seen over the concrete wall. Other children stood scattered about. It was cold.

'Where are *you* from?' said a fat boy with a red boil on his cheek. I told him I was from Trooperslane and he wanted to know where I was living. I told him it was down on the beach and he asked me the house's name. When I told him it was called The Bungalow, he said that because they were all bungalows, it was a stupid name. Then he wanted to know the number. I told him thirteen and that this was my father's lucky number.

'Well, your da's wrong, so he is. It's bad luck. My uncle changed his to a 12A.' There was no answer to that, so I stayed silent along with my desk mate. Then we all sucked the last dregs of milk, making as loud a noise as we could; the others, too, took up the loud sucking noise until every drop of milk was gone.

As I was placing my bottle back in the milk crate, a skinny girl in a kilt confronted me.

'What's your name, wee boy?'

'Ross.'

'What kind of a name is that?' I couldn't answer.

'I'm Nancy. Is he your friend?' she asked, looking suspiciously at Creighton.

At lunchtime, the whole playground was taken up with a football match between the end walls. Two piles of stones scraped together by hand each day marked the goals and an old grey tennis ball was produced. The match was fast and furious. I watched from the corner as the big boys fought over the tiny ball. Nancy came over.

'That Creighton, he's not right in the head,' she said.

'He was sticking glass into me,' I said, watching a group standing round a game of marbles in the other corner of the playground.

'He's not right in the head, him,' she repeated, solemnly tapping her forehead with a forefinger.

'I'm on over to the marbles. Are you coming?'

We waited for a lull in the fury of the match, and pushed through the circle of onlookers to two boys who were playing beside a large puddle. A rough circle had been scored in the tarmac and they were taking it in turns to try to knock out small glass marbles with a larger one. The match was ending: first one, then the other marble in the ring was knocked out.

'Good man, Bert,' someone called out to the winner, a burly, grinning boy with a front tooth missing. I liked the look of him.

'I'm next!' said a voice and Creighton pushed through just as raindrops fell into the big puddle.

'OK,' said the boy called Bert, looking up at the sky. 'We've just time before the rain.'

They each put a marble in the circle and another boy put his hand in his pocket and took out a penny.

'Heads or harps?' he said, flicking the coin.

'Heads!' said Creighton.

'Harps, then!' said Bert squinting at the coin on the wet ground. He took a big glass marble with a rainbow running through it and scooted it along the ground, but it missed. Creighton put his hand in his pocket, took it out closed and pitched his from knee height.

'It's a ball bearing!' someone said as the steel ball smashed the rainbow marble to pieces. The little group went quiet, and then a chorus of protest went up: 'That's not fair, so it's not.'

'That's not a real marley.'

But the rain was coming down and we all ran for the hallway. There we stood looking out at the thick slanted rain through which we could just see the footballers standing in the concrete shelter across the playground.

SOON, during playground time, I began to drift on the fringes of the big match with other outsiders – Rodger Lundy and Derek Gracey. The three of us had nothing in common except that we didn't like football, which dominated the playground, and we stood idly talking while the battle for the small ball raged around us. Occasionally a player would stumble into our little group, making us withdraw. Rodger's ma ran the ice-cream shop in Carrick and Derek's family were Holy Joes and so he had to go to Sunday school twice. Sometimes Creighton would join us. One day we had been working in the school garden and Rodger showed me how to make a 'sandwich'.

'Look,' he said, rubbing earth off two scallions and a radish, 'you wrap them in a lettuce leaf and,' he crunched up the green sandwich, 'brilliant!'

I tried it – it didn't taste half-bad – then we both watched Creighton who, without rubbing the earth off, crunched his sandwich.

'Jesus, you're supposed to take the roots of the scallions!' But heedless, he was already making another and, as he munched, was already making a third.

'He's just hungry,' Rodger said, 'His ma isn't in most of the time and his da's at sea.'

Once I saw Creighton's mother in the village street gossiping with another woman in her doorway. They stood, arms folded, engrossed in their conversation when a car with three nuns passed by. The woman in the door paused and spat on the ground three times. Then they resumed talking.

Sometimes at lunchtime, Mr Wylie, the headmaster, would wander round the playground. One day he saw a classmate of mine, Isobel, crying. He asked her what was wrong.

'Please sir, Billy McCallion threw an apple doot at me. My ear's hurt!' she sobbed.

'An apple doot? What's an apple doot?'

Isobel said nothing. I knew, as did she, that Mr Wylie was well aware that an apple doot was the local dialect for an apple core. I had noticed that the teachers would not use local colloquialisms. The radio didn't use our words either, but everyone knew the BBC always told the truth. At teatime the six bongs of Big Ben would sound.

'This is the BBC Home Service. Here is the news …'

In the mornings I was wakened by the music box pling-plonging of 'The Soldier's Song' from Radio Athlone. We were the only family for miles around that even knew where southern Irish radio was on the dial. This was because my mother, as a girl in Devon, had often listened to the station.

One morning the BBC was on instead.

'Today, at half past seven, King George VI died peacefully in his sleep. The sadness of the nation …'

To me, the King seemed far away. All I knew about him was what my mother had told me: that he had a stammer and was a good man. As an infant, in the Model School at Carrick, my class had been given little paper Union Jacks and we were ferried out to line the main road outside the school as George VI's sister, the Princess Royal, passed by. We stood freezing for an hour, clutching our flags until the cortège appeared crawling along at a snail's pace. When finally we were signalled to wave our Union Jacks, our reward was the glimpse of a pale arm raised in the back window of an elegant black limousine.

Like BBC Northern Ireland, Radio Athlone had jigs and reels – fiddle music mainly but never bagpipes. The pipes were definitely ours and on summer evenings the Star of Eden pipe band practice could be heard down on the beach. I wanted to join the band but a boy in school told me I had to be in the junior Orange Order.

'Mum, can I join the Orange Order?'

She looked at me in horror.

'Ask your father!' she said shortly.

At teatime I was too nervous to ask.

'He wants to join the Orange Order, Tom.'

Father stopped eating, a piece of sausage on his fork in mid-air. Then he started laughing and had to put it back down on the plate. Mother was smiling broadly.

'Can I, Daddy?'

'Over my dead body. Don't tell your grandfather. He'd have a fit.'

'Why can't I?'

'Because we're not those kind of people,' Mother said.

MISS SLOAN, my teacher, was a buxom woman who always wore knitted cardigans. We usually began lessons with the Lord's Prayer, one line of which exercised my imagination: 'And forgive us our trespasses …'

I always thought of the notice up the road: 'Trespassers will be shot.'

'For thine is the Kingdom, the Power and the Glory for ever and ever. Amen.'

'Billy, where were you yesterday?'

'Please, Miss, the cows got out.'

'Ross, you were late this morning.'

'Please Miss, the sea tore up the road,' I would say. Then

she would nod and address the class: 'Right, children we'll test your Bible now.'

I had usually only half-learned my verses. Mother tried to help but the Bible bored her. I would stare at the dull black book Miss Sloan was holding open in her left hand; in the other was the cane. Then I would look up the line of pupils along the classroom wall; we had to learn ten verses a night. The teacher took up her cane and, pointing it at the first in the line, demanded the first verse. It was usually Bert. I would look up to the head of the queue, and count: I would be verse seven. Now, what was verse seven? Oh, yes it was … swish, swish went the cane through the air. Bert had failed. I would be verse six now unless Lily couldn't do hers, in which case I would be five. What was six? Oh yes – I remembered. Swish, swish. Lily would hold her hand, fighting back tears. The next four might manage their verses. Then I would be verse five – what's five I thought? The teacher loomed, cane twitching.

'In my Father's house are many mansions …' I said in a rush. I could only think of Mansion floor polish – my mother let me wear pads on my feet and polish the floor of the bungalow by skating over it. Stuck, I stared helplessly at the purple mountains on the wall map of Ireland: Macgilly-cuddy's Reeks.

' … mansions, *if* …' prompted the teacher.

'If it were not so, I would have told you,' I finished with an eye on the twitching cane. As the interrogation moved down the room, I stared at the map. Ireland was very big. I wondered why it was all broken down the left-hand side.

By late morning the stove would be bright orange with the heat when Miss Sloan relented and stopped feeding it coal.

'Goodness, it's hot in here,' she would say, as if realizing it for the first time and, opening a window, she would prop it up with the blackboard duster.

ONE EASTER, Miss Sloan had given us out Dr Barnardo's Easter egg cards to collect donations. In the centre of the card was the image of an egg on which donors wrote their names. My mother was keen for me to collect a lot of money for the charity and she came up with an unexpected idea – that I should ask Miss Higgins for a donation. Mother got me to write a letter about collecting for Dr Barnardo's and post it to the big house at the end of the beach. After a few days I received a reply that the gate would be left open for me on the following Saturday.

It was a sunny morning when I entered and walked through the silent garden between squares of flowers and huge jungle-like plants. Suddenly, rounding the end of a hedge, I saw the mysterious Miss Higgins. She was gardening on her hands and knees and wearing a large floppy straw hat. Her manner was soft and gentle and, as she weeded, we talked of what my father did for a living. When I said he was a writer, she looked taken aback. But I was used to that now, for it either provoked perplexity or incredulity. She gave me a ten shilling note, signed the card with a scribble, and I left in triumph.

Encouraged by this I decided to try the new neighbour, Jackie McCosh, who lived near Miss Higgins' paling fence in an old goods truck minus wheels.

When I knocked at the door, there was no reply, so I gently pushed it open. On the table was a tin of Heinz baked beans with an open jagged lid and a spoon sticking up out of it. A small, wiry man in a dirty vest and cap was sitting on a box by the fire, cleaning a rifle. Suddenly he pointed it at me.

'Don't shoot!'

'Oh, I had you there.' He laughed. 'Come in, come in. Are you collecting for something?'

As I entered, I stepped over a long plank, which stretched from door to fire. The farther end was burning in the stove.

'Would you give that plank a kick into the fire? The end's near burned out,' he said.

My kick was not enough, so I bent, lifted the heavy piece of timber and shoved it farther into the flames.

'It's Ross, isn't it – Tom's lad? Are you collecting for something?'

I nodded. He handed me sixpence. I handed him the Barnardo's card telling him he had to sign.

'Write my name for me – John McCosh.'

'IS HE any relation to you?' said a thin boy at milk-time as the red-faced boy called Bert passed with a curt nod towards me. 'He's Skelton too.'

Creighton, as usual was standing beside me; he was beginning to be annoying. Wherever I went, he went too, until one day I had too much and told him to leave me alone. After that, the glass treatment began in earnest: at every opportunity he stabbed the air under the desk at my knees with a piece of broken glass.

One milk-time I stood fascinated by the goal watching Billy Irvine, the star playground goalkeeper. To save the ball, he would throw himself headlong on the tarmac as if his life depended on it. In later years he went on to play for Burnley.

Standing in a group watching the match, but really hiding from my tormentor, I saw the ball was very near. A violent rush of players came hurtling at the goal. Creighton spotted me and headed straight for me, walking in front of Bert who was defending the goal.

Billy could not save the ball, which hit the wall. Goal!

White-faced, Bert turned and hit Creighton a thump in the chest. The players stopped to watch.

'Fight! Fight!' someone shouted.

'If. You. Ever do that …' Bert said, pushing the boy back.

'You're yolkey,' Creighton sneered.

Bert hit him in the mouth and he fell back dazed on to the tarmac, blood on his teeth.

'And leave my cousin alone!' said Bert, turning away. The boy looked up at his back, perplexed.

'Who?'

'Him,' said Bert, turning and nodding towards me. I went red. When I got home, I asked my mother if Bert was my cousin but she said to ask Father.

'Is Bert Skelton any relation to us?' I said.

Father went into a long account of the family connection until my mind glazed over. When I regained consciousness he was saying that he supposed Bert and I must be second cousins. I was thrilled! I had a real cousin here in Eden. Soon Bert and I began walking down the lane from school together.

AT THE AGE of ten, when we were in senior class at Eden Primary, Mr Wylie taught us. He liked to come up behind one of the girls in class and suddenly tickle them, making them squirm and giggle. In the playground one day, I asked Nancy and Ada why he did this and they replied that it was because he was a dirty old man. I told them they must like it if they laughed. At this they bristled.

'He tickles you too – and you laugh.' It was true. I blushed.

Nancy was tricky like that. One time a few of us went to the pictures. I was beside Nancy, who was giggling with Ada on the other side. During the picture Nancy whispered in my ear: 'Put your hand on my leg.'

'No, I will not.'

'Go on – I dare you.'

I had tried to ignore her; what could she be up to? I had no idea. Why would I want to put my hand on her leg?

'Put your hand on my leg,' Nancy persisted. 'Go on.'

I gave in and put my hand on her skinny thigh. It felt like nothing. Then I took it away. She started talking to her friends on the other side.

'He did not!' Ada said, shocked.

'Ross, did you put your hand on Nancy's leg?' Ada asked. Two usherettes' torches spotlighted the conversation.

'Be quiet or get out,' said the one with long blonde hair.

'Get out yourself,' said Ada, 'or I'll tell our Billy about you and wee Sammy.'

'Well, keep it down then.' The torch snapped off; the other torch came closer. It was an older teenage girl, who used to be in the chip shop.

'Is that you, Nancy Blair? Does your mother know you're at the pictures?' she said flicking the torch to and fro across their faces. The girls fell quiet except for a few nudges and giggles.

The next day in school I started to speak to Isobel at milk-time, but she turned away from me, then turned back.

'Did you put your hand on Nancy Blair's leg?'

I said it had been her idea.

'You're a dirty wee boy, so you are.'

It was some time before things came back to normal. Shortly after that incident, I was coming down the lane from school bringing Rodger Lundy home to play. We were walking down the lane when we met Nancy going to her friend Edith's house. Edith had a skipping rope round her neck, and her satchel tied to the end.

'Since when were you two friends?' I said, nudging Rodger and smirking.

'Since when were you two friends?' mimicked Edith. 'Nancy says you felt her leg at the pictures.' Angrily I grabbed the skipping rope and pulled — hard. Edith's face went red and she fell to the ground. I stood looking on in disbelief. The rope had been wound round her neck. I hadn't known. Rodger got the rope off and Edith soon recovered.

'I'm going to tell your ma,' she said in a shaky voice.

'You nearly killed her. Edie could have been dead!' said Nancy venomously.

'That thing at the pictures — that was your idea,' I said. Nancy said nothing and ran off to catch up with Edith.

'It wasn't your fault,' said Rodger, but I wasn't listening. There would be trouble.

When we arrived at the beach, Edith's mother was already there and, with a black look to me, walked off fast, arms folded.

'Ross is not playing today,' my mother said to Rodger, who left. When he had gone, she turned on me.

'Edith's mother said you tried to strangle her and that her face turned purple and she could have died.'

I told her I didn't know the rope had been actually wound around her neck.

'That's it! Go to bed. And you'll have no tea!'

Nobody was sent to bed as a punishment in our neighbourhood but I was used to her English ways and felt lucky to get off so lightly. As I waited in bed, I knew my father would be a different matter.

'What'll Father say?'

'I'll explain to him,' she said, but I was still worried and lay there in the late afternoon waiting for him to come home. When he arrived I could hear them arguing. Then, when I could hear my mother's voice pleading less and less and my father's deep voice prevailing, I knew I was lost.

I was pulled out of bed and could see Father was about to give me a terrible hiding, exactly what I had expected.

The next thing I can recall is lying on the floor and my mother bending over me.

'Are you all right, darling?'

I had fainted. Father stood looking uncertain, while Mother handed me a glass of water. When I had recovered, he led me out the back door.

'Where are you going?' Mother said, white-faced.

'He's going to Edith's father to apologize.'

Father took the back lane instead of going past the bungalows on the beach, so I knew he didn't want to be seen. At Edith's house he took me by the ear and led me up the sloping path to her house. Her father answered the door. He took one look at me, head held on one side by the ear, shocked. Father made me apologize, but I could see that Edith's father was sorry for me.

'Well, Edith's all right – no harm done.' Her father made light of it and, looking at my father as if he was a madman, smiled guiltily at me.

Father let go my ear and we walked home in silence along the green lane behind the bungalow roofs. When we got home and he had calmed down, we all had a silent dinner. Halfway through, my father paused and spoke:

'If you can't learn morality the easy way, then you can learn it the hard way. You will go to church for one year!'

And so, from the next Sunday, I took the bus to Carrick.

I loved the walk to church through the town on a summer's morning for, since I was always late, the streets were already empty. The near-deserted town was filled with the pealing of big bells and, as I looked up, I smiled to see all the racing pigeons out for a fly. Sunday was open loft day for all the pigeon-fanciers of the town and I always took my time on the way to church, following my own route to look at the pigeon lofts. My favourite could just be seen over the large wooden gate of a back yard. Behind that was a wall of small pigeon houses, each of different design. I loved to stare at them for it reminded me of something I had seen in the pictures. The Gaumont Newsreel once had an item about Postman Cheval, from the south of France, who each day collected a few rocks in his postbag and started building a strange and wonderful palace.

Carrick Congregational Church was built of red brick and glowed in the sunshine. The reason it was our church was because after the war my father and his two brothers agreed to choose one church each and he got the Congregationalists. My parents never attended although they knew the clergyman.

I sat alone behind the mayor and his wife. There were four hymns: three with readings between, then the sermon followed by the last hymn. There was no clock in the church, but the time passed somehow. Finally came the long awaited blessing and the organist struck up happy rousing music as the bolts of the high doors were pulled and the morning sunlight streamed in.

As we stepped out blinking into the sunshine streets, I would look up at the sky. Not many pigeons now; just the occasional solitary bird crossing with only a few wing strokes. I would walk to the bus stop and be back home for Sunday dinner.

I WAS soon to discover that the beach was lonely in winter, for there were few people of my age nearby. If I sat too long indoors, Mother would demand that I 'do something'. It was then I usually went looking for driftwood along the shore. Sometimes I would just go down to the beach and stare at the brown waves spewing white on to the sand, which were, for me, an inrush of jostling sheep. Twelve miles up the lough, beyond Carrickfergus, Harland and Wolff's shipyard gantries could be glimpsed in the haze. At that time, the early 1950s, the shipyard had a lot of work. As each ship was launched down the slipway and hit the water, there would be a rush of debris along with it – mostly offcuts of timber, which had gathered while the vessel was fitted out. Whenever there was a rough sea, this flotsam was washed up along the shores of the lough and the direction of the wind and tides favoured our stretch of beach. Much of the wood was plywood, some of it Formica-covered and for years we had such a piece as a kitchen chopping board. But the most sought after pieces were the twelve-foot pine planks, for if you got one it could be taken to Crowe's sawmill where they would slice it into neat boards for you.

As I ventured out the back door into the winter weather, I would throw a hessian sack on my wooden cart with its old pram wheels. Rounding the bungalow corner I usually felt the force of a strong breeze. If it was raining, I took one corner of the sack and pushed it into the other, which made a kind of bonnet to keep off the rain.

As I dragged the cart behind me, crunching down the shingle towards the tide, my eyes would swivel among the seaweed. Brightly coloured tins contrasted with the ruin of tangleweed; pieces of wood; lots of bottles – Dutch, Irish and Russian. Clear bottles usually contained messages from Jehovah's Witnesses destined for the cannibal inhabitants of the South Seas. They were in six languages and had been launched from just across the lough by religious zealots. Sometimes a dead dog with rotten teeth grimaced from the seaweed.

I would slouch, head down, along the edge of the vast stretches of the low tide, with only a murmur of sea noises from the ebb reaching my strained ears. I would wander on with that peculiar bleak boredom I always felt, occasionally looking up at a gull sliding on the wind. The gulls, I thought, were always what gave the final touch of desolation to the beach in winter.

When I had rounded the Point, our sea wall, which sheltered the bay, I sank into a steady stumbling rhythm over the rocks. Occasionally I stopped to pick up a chunk of wood and dropped it in the sack, or hesitated over a piece considering its worth, or puzzle at a knotted contraceptive. Bert told me that they were called French letters but neither of us knew exactly their purpose. Here and there, good boards or planks would be laid up, well above the tide line, to show they were 'booked'. To take one and be discovered was asking for a terrible wall of silence from the other beachcombers, notably from the Irons family, the Mafia of beachcombers. Three or four brothers took it in turns to cover the beach each day and woe betide anyone who helped themselves to their wood. On one particular occasion, my father told me he had heard shouting outside. He had found Willie Smith arguing with one of the Irons sons. The old man had picked up an axe and was swinging it round his head as the Irons boy lifted the disputed plank to use as a battering ram. It was only when Jackie McCosh emerged carrying his rifle and threatened to shoot that the younger man backed off.

Eventually, often in driving rain, my rambles would take me past the Lobster Stone, a huge rock far out over the wet sand where, if I could find no more wood, I would switch to the Larne Harbour railway line. Carefully choosing the line facing any oncoming trains, my feet perfectly attuned to stepping from sleeper to sleeper, in half an hour I would be looking down into Cloughan Bay, a deserted inlet where the shore shelved deeply. It was a soundless place where nothing stirred, not even a gull. I always thought even the gulls would not dare to go there, which made me feel uneasy, so that within a few minutes I usually retreated as if from the Isle of the Dead.

One day I had climbed down into the steep-sided bay and walked along the shore. It was slightly eerie and, as I was thinking I should not be there, I saw in the distance a long, black straight object on some rocks. Close up, I saw it was a full-length piece of wet timber, resting precariously on the points of the rocks. I had found my first 'plank'. I hoisted it on to my right shoulder and climbed back up to the railway line. With a backward glance at the silent bay, I started carrying the plank home along the railway.

When I arrived home, I heard hammering and the splintering of wood. No one came to admire my plank. The yard was full of broken timber and the back door was open. Inside, wielding a claw hammer, Father was tearing down the partition that separated the bathroom from the kitchen.

'Mind Ross, Tom!' Mother shouted as the remains of the wall fell.

'Fool boy. Bring me the sledgehammer.'

I came back puffing, hardly able to carry it and set it at his feet. As we watched, he lifted the sledge and hit the iron bath: the side fell on the wooden floor. I gaped; I had no idea it would be so easy. A few more choice blows and the big bath was in shards on the floor. We carried out the pieces and piled them under the hedge. Then Father pulled up the waste pipe from the floor, leaving a hole. After Mother swept the remaining debris down the hole, my father nailed a square piece of wood over it.

'Tom, won't we trip over that?' said Mother.

'It's fine,' he said, but I thought it didn't look right. In fact this was typical of Father's slapdash repairs. I remember one morning at Trooperslane when I came downstairs to find Father had sawed off all the legs of the easy chairs. Mother was standing by looking doubtful as he nailed straight boards to the chair sides so that they were reclined. Greater comfort was achieved by his efforts, but the chairs looked terrible for when Father found he had not enough nails, he hammered in woodscrews, which left a scarred surface.

The patched hole in the floor was to be with us for years and our visitors were usually perplexed when their chair could not be moved smoothly aside or closer to the table. Eventually they always peered down to see what was obstructing their chair legs and would see the square patch.

THERE WERE ONLY TWO real carpenters on the beach: Willie Smith, the beach patriarch, and Sammy Calderwood, who worked in the shipyard. One day I bought a ruler in Coles' shop and I kept it in my leather school bag. When I looked into Willie's workshop on my way back from school, he saw it sticking out.

'Give us a look at that,' he said, taking it and, putting it up to the light, he looked along its edge.

'It's not straight!' he pronounced, putting it in the vise and taking down a large wooden plane. Gently, he shaved a few slivers off it and then held it up.

'That's more Protestant-looking,' he said, handing it back to me. I was disappointed he had not made lots of shavings, but since that day I saw him like a god: he had corrected something that I had thought perfect.

Sammy was short and muscular with an oily quiff in his short black hair. He was a carpenter in the Queen's Island, as he called it. I wanted to be like him and each Saturday morning I went along the beach to help him. He showed me how to saw straight, hold a chisel, rule lines and hammer in nails. When I made a mistake, he was patient until I got it right, unlike Father.

The bungalows were often in need of repair and Sammy seemed to openly savour any opportunities to fix his house. He would slowly accumulate the materials and on a Saturday morning would begin work. He had a real affection for the wood and tools and seemed to relish every hammer blow and every bite of his freshly sharpened saw.

Next door to Sammy was Fred Grey, who made a living by buying and selling. No one was quite sure what he bought or sold, but he eventually struck gold. He acquired hundreds of empty caustic soda tin barrels from a factory and, in his garden, chiselled off the circular ends. Then he cut the welded joint to make a metal rectangle six feet by four. Since they had to be cleaned, he hit on the idea of washing them in the sea. So, every morning as I went to school he could be seen in his gumboots, standing in the waves scrubbing what he called his 'tins'. With one foot he held down the tin while vigorously using a yard brush on it to get rid of the caustic soda. After all this cleaning, Fred's glistening tins were ready for sale at half a crown each – an inexpensive substitute for corrugated iron. They sold quickly, mostly to farmers building cheap out-houses, and Sammy bought some to extend his workshop.

Fred soon had made enough to buy the first television set on the beach. It was June 1953, just in time for the coronation of Elizabeth II, and nearly all the beach neighbours crammed into Fred's bungalow to watch. All you could see on it was a snowstorm and fragments of the royal event but everyone was delighted that they had witnessed it at all. We children would watch cowboy pictures and, even if the screen was fuzzy, we could hear the gunfire and that was enough for us.

Fred's brother, who had been recently unemployed, came to live with him. With canary-coloured waistcoats and a pipe clenched in his teeth, he soon acquired the nickname 'Puffer' Grey. All he ever seemed to do was strut about the place looking prosperous. One day, Sammy borrowed a paintbrush from Puffer; it was encrusted and dirty. He cleaned it thoroughly before using it and returned it looking like new.

'Why did you bother?' I said, knowing the brush's original condition.

'To make his ears burn,' Sam replied.

ALL THE BUNGALOWS were up on blocks so that if there were a very high tide, which the breakwater could not hold back, the sea, instead of going into the houses, would flow underneath them.

Our next-door neighbours, Jack and Lily, had a magnificent breakwater. He had used his old lorry to fetch railway sleepers and boulders with which he and his wife had fashioned a substantial battlement against the sea. Years later when I asked my mother why the couple had no children, she told me that any time Lily was pregnant she would work on the breakwater, lifting heavy stones until she miscarried.

Our own defence against the sea did not interest my father and was a flimsy affair built by Mother and myself. Since our house was the one closest to the sea, we were the most vulnerable so, after a bad storm, we had fashioned a kind of a frame from large rocks and then forgot about it.

Following the death of a relation of my father's, a horse and cart arrived one day at the gate. The cart was filled with books, mostly religious – including about a hundred Bibles. The non-religious books my mother piled up in the outdoors lavatory. When you sat on the seat in there, close to your face was a wall of books high to the ceiling. Sometimes if I started to pull one out, the edifice would tilt threateningly overhead, and I would have to push the book back in again.

One book I did manage to extract was *Goldsmith's Animated Nature* and when I turned to the entry written under 'lobster', I laughed out loud as I read that to change its shell, the lobster turns onto its back, screams three times and sheds its shell.

Having no room to store the Bibles indoors, Mother had dumped them secretly in the breakwater and covered them with stones. I had no knowledge of this so that on the morning after the next storm I was astonished to find, strewn, all along the beach, hundreds of sodden pages of scripture. Lily (who never went to church) would not speak to my mother after that and in fact did not speak to us for several years. Sometimes when my mother and I were walking the path along by the bungalows, we would meet her and she would pass by, stony-faced.

ONE DAY BERT AND I were standing in the lane. As we looked up the hill to the village a figure appeared freewheeling down the dusty lane. Soon we saw the tall thin cyclist was wearing a flowing floral dress. One hand was on the handlebars, the other held on to a wide-brimmed straw hat.

'Good afternoon, boys,' she greeted us as she passed.

'Who is that?' I said, staring after her.

'That's the Duchess,' said Bert, grinning.

'But what's her name?'

'I don't know. She's the Duchess, that's all I know. They arrived last week. She's tall and he's a midget.'

It wasn't long before my mother got to know the Duchess, actually Lettie Todhunter from County Mayo. Mother soon began visiting her bungalow across the railway line and eventually one day I went with her.

At the door I asked my mother if the woman was a real duchess, but she gave me a scornful look just as the door opened. It was the Commander, her husband, a tiny, wiry man whose greeting was lost in the rush of a passing train.

From my corner I looked at Lettie's spaniel-like eyes and drooping features, which reminded me of pictures of kings and queens in my history book. I drank a lemonade while the two women sipped tea from two orange Bakelite cups. After chatting about the weather, Mother set down her cup and Lettie picked it up, peering into it. As she began turning it this way and that, examining the pattern of the tea leaves, I noticed the huge rings on her long fingers.

I looked idly around the Todhunter's kitchen. High on a shelf sat a big silver container with a tap and beside it a packet of Typhoo tea. My mother remarked on the large silver receptacle on the shelf. Lettie explained that it was a Russian samovar that had belonged to her great-aunt. She frowned into the cup, then started to speak, but a sudden heavy shower drummed on the wooden roof and I could not hear what was said. The rain stopped. Lettie was speaking:

'...there's a mountain no, more like an iceberg.'

'Goodness! That sounds frightful,' said Mother, shocked. Lettie started, as if woken from a dream, apologizing that she sometimes got carried away.

'Can I have my tea leaves read?' I piped up.

Mother told me not to be ridiculous but Lettie said she would read my hand. I moved to a stool near the sofa, she bent over my fingers, examined my palm and told me I had a long lifeline.

'Perhaps we should go,' said Mother quickly. I was annoyed. I had wanted to hear more, much more.

'Is it true you talk to dead people?' I suddenly asked Lettie. Mother demanded I apologize, but Lettie just said I was too young to be thinking about such things and at Mother's word we got up to leave.

Outside everything was wet and fresh. Mother was obviously angry.

'I was so embarrassed in there. You're never to say things like that again!'

'Well, you didn't even pay!'

'Pay? What do you mean?'

'Bert's Ma paid when the Duchess brought his uncle back from the dead. He told me she paid a pound.'

We walked home in silence along the cinder path.

BERT AND I were becoming friends. One day we were kicking a rusty tin down the lane and we had just reached Lockhart's shop when he told me he was going to get rabbits from Big Alec. I asked my mother if I could get them too.

'Ask your father,' she replied.

'What, in the name of God do you want rabbits for?' said Father.

'Tom, he really wants them. Bert's getting them.'

So, with money in our pockets, we went up the lane to buy rabbits.

Alec was a farmer, a big man who always wore a cap, even indoors. Some said he wore it in bed. The farmer positioned himself in a large wooden captain's chair and looked around the kitchen while his sister brought us Cochrane's lemonade.

'Boys, I've no rabbits,' he announced.

Shocked, we stared at him. We had built our whole case for rabbits because of Alec having them.

'I only keep pigeons now. Rabbits don't do anything except eat. A few nice pigeons about the place are just the thing; always something to look at.'

At first we weren't persuaded, but as big Alec sang the praises of pigeons we were slowly won over and when we left his house we were full of it – nothing would do us but to have pigeons. My father looked brighter at the prospect of pigeons and agreed. Bert's Da, Robert, told me to buy two orange boxes, which I did. All week I stared at the tropical pictures on them, pictures of palm trees and blue seas. On Saturday morning my father showed me how to join together the boxes to make a pigeon loft.

I named my first two birds Snowy and Joey: Snowy was white, Joey, the hen, speckled black and white. They were a high-flying breed called Tipplers and soon flew so high they quickly became two dots. Pigeons were to become an important part of our lives.

EVERY FEW DAYS the bread van arrived outside the front gate and 'Ormeau' Joe climbed down from his purple van. The baker wore a beige coat, had a turn in one eye and always wore a hat which he was forever taking off and putting back on. I always noticed his strange, icy blue eyes. He opened the back doors of the van.

'How many would you like today, Missus?' he always said,

and Mother would reel off a list: batch loaves, soda farls, treacle bread and potato bread. He would reach deep into the dark shelving with his hooked pole and a wooden tray would fly swiftly out into the daylight. Then Mother was handed loaves and the tray whizzed out of sight. 'Will that be all, Missus?' he would say. 'How's himself? Reading. God, he's a great man for reading. How many books do you think he's read now? Must be thousands.'

On one particular Saturday morning, Bert and myself had been watching Fred scrub the caustic soda off his tins in the sea, but we soon grew bored and when Joe arrived we went to watch him.

'Away with you!' Joe shouted, pretending to be angry and we ran, laughing, away down the shingle. The van's back doors were left swinging open as he levered himself up into the cab and started along the pathway above the shore. While he attended to another customer, we started playing on the road again and as he drove off, towards us, he accelerated.

Pretending to lose control, Joe covered his face with his hands as if the van was about to crash. Well used to his sense of humour, we ran off the path down the beach screaming. Joe's eyes were still covered when the van, doors swinging, hit a stone and lurched on to the shingle, then careered towards the water, trays and bread scattering over the beach.

Fred, scrubbing his tins, took one look and ran out of the water and up the beach. Still going, the van plunged up to its axles in the sea.

There it sat, the tide silently lapping against the radiator. The baker slowly climbed down into the water as Bert and I watched in disbelief. Natasha barked and my father, hearing the dog, came outside, holding a book open in one hand and a mug of tea in the other. Joe stood, in his baker's coat, up to his waist in water facing out to sea, then he turned round and slowly waded ashore. My father was joined by Willie Smith and then Lily Evans; I noticed she had a bruised eye. Oddly enough she would speak to Father but not Mother and, arms folded, she stood watching with him.

'He always was a bit touched, Joe,' said Willie, 'but he's a good soul.'

'A good soul?' said Lily. 'It's a miracle that lunatic didn't get one of the children.'

'My Da says he's not right in the head, him,' said Bert.

'Here comes Lady Muck,' said Lily as the tall figure of Lettie appeared, riding her high bicycle, dress blowing in the breeze, one hand on her large hat.

'That poor man. I believe he's only out of Purdysburn this week,' she said.

Eventually Joe reached the little group and our neighbours faded away, leaving just Father and myself.

'C'mon in, Joe,' my father said to the soaked baker. 'We'll get you dry,' and he led him round to the back door.

Mother handed Joe two towels, then went to find some dry clothes. She returned with old grey flannels over her arm and an old shirt of Father's which she handed to Joe.

I went outside to have a look at the van in the sea. The beach was engulfed in a storm of screeching seagulls that had found the contents of the van. One flew overhead carrying a potato farl in its beak; Natasha ran among them barking, not really wanting to catch any but enjoying the noisy confusion.

After a while I came in just as the bedroom door was opening. I stopped open-mouthed staring at a man in a flight lieutenant's battledress, medal ribbons in lines over the breast pocket. Joe was wearing my father's old uniform. It made me feel peculiar.

'What do you think?' Joe said, giving a mock salute. Father sat down suddenly and Mother, who had appeared with two mugs of tea, nearly dropped them at the sight.

'Just kidding,' said Joe, taking off the jacket which my mother, embarrassed, took from him.

The three of them sat in the porch for some time without speaking, looking out the large window at the dispersing gulls. Father looked pale.

'I'll catch the train now,' Joe said and left.

THERE WAS no doubt my father had been badly affected by the war. It wasn't just the nightmares from which he woke shouting, or even the yearly malaria attacks, when he would be in delirium for several days; it was his nerves. Whenever there was a sudden noise or unexpected news, he would show the whites of his eyes. On the times when he gave me a beating, I would look into his eyes and see pure terror there. It was as if he was the one being beaten – not me.

In those early days at the beach he was mostly in a bad mood; he was like a man with perpetual toothache and he flew off the handle without warning.

Bendy Mahood, so named because one leg was deformed, drove a donkey and cart. One day outside the house he drove it over my bike that was lying in the road, buckling the back wheel. I left the wheel in the front garden. When Father got home he saw it and, enraged, gave me a hiding. In vain, my mother tried to intervene in this storm of punishment but she had to wait until it died down before telling him it had not been my fault – that Bendy had done it. He looked at me. I had dried my eyes and was sitting quietly at the table.

'Sorry, boy,' he said.

Father was soon to find another way of soothing his troubled mind. One day after school the postman came bumping on his bike along the stony path to the house. He handed over a heavy book-shaped parcel that I laid on the table. Every now and then I fingered it: it looked important. Then, when my father came in from work, he opened it. Inside, were two brown volumes, one of which he started to read, standing by the table. The family had to wait half an hour to start tea.

He was still reading when I went to bed. The next morning, before going to school, I peeped at the brown cover: 'C.G. Jung' I read, *The Collected Works, Volume Three, The Psychogenesis of Mental Disease.* On my way up the lane to school, I wondered about the book. In later years my father confessed to me that he had been having a breakdown and had bought the Jung books to try and cure himself.

MA AND PA, having left Sunnylands, were now settled in our old house at Trooperslane. Sadie, while carrying on with her teaching, looked after them.

I remember the first visit Mother and I made to our old suburban home. The train we took was drawn by the big, ugly engine. It was the only diesel on the line and my friend Mark and I had never liked it because, unlike the steam engines, it had no number for us to write down. Andy, the stationmaster, was on the platform when we arrived and as we approached, he was, as usual, whistling between his teeth.

'How's the beach? There was a bit of a wind last night,' he smiled, watching Mother's face.

'Oh we're getting on fine,' she said cheerily, meeting Andy's eye. Recently, the buffeting of the wind had been like huge soft punches on the wooden house. There was no need to go into details. Mother had already learned that much about

Ulster: whatever you say, say nothing. Andy waved the green flag and the diesel droned loudly out of the station.

After the first meeting with Ma and Sadie in the parlour, I ran upstairs to see my old bedroom where my mother and I had cut out magazine pictures and pasted them all over one wall in a huge collage. I burst through the door: my wall of colours was gone! Even Mr Bates' paintings of galleons had vanished. I ran downstairs to Ma.

'What happened to my pictures?'

'Oh, the painter stripped them off,' she added absent-mindedly, 'before we could stop him.'

'Your Granda's in the kitchen. Go and say hello,' said Sadie. I ran into the kitchen, where Pa was hidden behind the *Belfast News Letter*.

'Ross's here, Pa,' she called. The paper dropped.

'Hey boy!' he barked with a grin, then returned to reading. I went back in the parlour where Ma was holding court:

'I will not see Tom as long as he has that disgusting beard,' she pronounced.

'Well, he won't shave,' my mother said, looking cross.

By the time we left, she and I were both in a bad mood and as the train passed Courtaulds Factory, which my father had helped build, I could contain myself no longer.

'How could they take down all our pictures – even Mister Bates' watercolours?'

'Hatred!' she said with finality.

Mother and I visited every few weeks and, on leaving, I always got a half crown from Ma – except once.

'Well, goodbye,' chorused Ma and Sadie, but I was not to be thwarted.

'Where's my money?'

There was a shocked silence. Ma looked embarrassed.

'Apologize at once!' snapped my mother, red-faced. When we got home, Father was told and gave me a half-hearted telling-off.

Probably the lowest point of the relationship between my mother and Ma came over a literary competition. Mother had entered myself and Joss for a competition in *The Times Literary Supplement* to find new words for 'The Twelve Days of Christmas'. We had done a beach version: 'Twelve crabs a-crawling' all the way down to 'And a lobster in a blue shell.' It had been published and when I came into the parlour she was showing Ma our new words in print.

'No, he did it himself,' my mother was insisting.

'Your mother did it, didn't she?' Ma urged. I didn't know what to say, for she had been there all the time it was being done.

'She did it,' I burst out, even though I knew it wasn't strictly true.

'Ross! You know I only helped a bit,' Mother said, embarrassed. Ma looked triumphant. On the way home on the train my mother was quiet.

'Why didn't you stick up for me?'

'I don't know, Mum.'

The truth was we were both afraid of Ma and, although she doted on me, I didn't dare cross her. In retrospect, I think Ma punished my mother because in some obscure way she blamed her for what my father had become: an impoverished writer, rather than a clergyman. Interestingly, Pa's father, known as Tin Hat, had been a bearded lay preacher, often being invited into houses where he gave kitchen sermons. Father's beard also reminded Ma of the artisan classes and her own lowly origins.

As a young woman Ma had been a gifted dressmaker, much sought after by the big houses in the countryside around Carrickfergus. She would cycle for miles to these houses to take fittings. Eventually she had set up a small business in the town. Her plaque had read: Jeannie Ross, *Costumière*.

'*Costumière*? Just a bloody oul' dressmaker,' Pa would remark.

Pa was a like a fish out of water in the suburbs. No longer able to roam the fields with a shotgun, looking for rabbits, nor able to shoot clay pigeons with his cronies, he was at a loose end.

The first sign that he had conceded to the alien environment at Trooperslane came as a shock to me. I had been up in my old bedroom and looked out the window down to the log beside the railway where Mark and I used to play. It had half gone! Sawn up! For Mark and me it had been a ship, a lorry, a plane. At one point we had even been persuaded by an older boy that, inside, the log was full of tiny people.

I knew immediately Pa had done it, for the style was identical to what I recalled from Sunnylands: the cut slabs were lying ready for the hatchet.

'It gives him something to do,' said Sadie when I asked. 'Otherwise, he just reads the paper mostly and goes out over the fields.'

We were walking slowly down the path towards the bridge. I followed and we stood above the river, listening to its music.

'I think it'll kill him, living here,' she said, her voice breaking and tears welling up in her eyes. I didn't know what to say, but sensed she was right.

On one of my occasional solo visits to Trooperslane, Ma, Sadie and I watched from the window as Pa went up the garden to turn over his rowing boat. It was clear he could not manage it. We pretended not to have seen his struggle when he came back down the garden and asked Sadie to give him a hand. But it wasn't just that. As time passed, the old man seemed to be living far behind his eyes and before long he became forgetful and astray in the head. That winter, he took to wandering at night in the fields around Trooperslane. Whenever he didn't return, Sadie would get a message to us and my father would take the motorbike over there and search the fields. Placing his fingers in his mouth, he would whistle as if calling for the dogs and Pa would then try to find him in the dark. They groped their way towards each other in the blackness, and then he led his father home.

'He's as strong as a horse, that man,' Father would say with resignation when anyone spoke of Pa's health. But before long the old man was bedridden and when the doctor proclaimed he was 'living off his muscle', we all knew he had not long to go.

After Pa's death in 1952, Ma and Sadie were always very glad to see me, especially Sadie, who seemed quieter then. My visits were an opportunity for Ma to keep track of Father, to whom she still never spoke as he refused to shave off his beard.

At that time I was doing a lot of carpentry, particularly in modifying the pigeon loft, and was trying to build up a collection of tools. During those Sunday visits, I was allowed to rummage through Pa's belongings, including his tools from the pantry at Sunnylands. For hours, I would happily sort through the old tools, rusty from lack of use but otherwise sound. I would pick out five or six items, such as a chisel, two drill bits and a saw, to take home. One day I discovered a banjo with no strings; another day, brass knuckledusters which I tried on but they were too big for my hand. I took them anyway. Ma always limited the amount I could carry away so that I would have to visit again soon. Then I would catch the train home and reveal my spoils.

'I'll take those!' Father would say and put them away out of sight. This upset me because he was hopeless with tools. I had been taught by Sammy up the beach and was appalled to see Father driving woodscrews in with a hammer or neglecting to sharpen saws or chisels. He had once ordered me to saw a six-foot board in half, lengthwise. Each day after school I did it for half an hour but the saw was so blunt, it took a whole week. Worst of all, he never put anything away, but just left them down where he had been working.

When I told Ma that he had been taking the tools I had collected, she claimed Pa had intended them especially for me. But then my father started doing the thing I dreaded. Pa's things, now supposedly mine, would reappear in the back yard on the large wooden bench covered with saws, chisels, drills, hammers, screwdrivers, nails, planes and bits of wood. The bench was open to the sky so when it rained they got soaked. After the rain I would examine the gentle rust stains forming as they dried. Sometimes I rubbed them off with a forefinger. Even today when I remind my brother of that bench, he shudders.

When it snowed, the snow lay thick on the tools and soft bumps covered the bench. I would watch the snow thaw and melt, dripping from the wooden bench into puddles below. In summer they dried off again and were used a lot in good weather but then they were laid aside during the slow descent into winter with its wind, rain and snow.

EVER SINCE PA'S death I had noticed my father was generally in a better mood. He often whistled and he also drove faster. One day I found him in the yard using a large spanner to unbolt the sidecar from the motorbike. This allowed him to ride at greater speed. He took the motorbike to work and one of my jobs was to open the railway gate on his return in the evening so that he could ride straight down over the lines to the beach. When I heard the engine's noise coming down the lane beside Loughside farm, I would run up to the railway line and stand waiting by the rusty gate as the Larne boat train passed and watch the back end of the carriages bucking away down the line. My father would soon burst into view, snorting and bouncing along the stony lane. The Hallion, his name for the bike, was a 1936 Ariel Red Hunter – a competition bike. I would hold the gate open ready to let him cross the lines but, though I waved him over, he looked both ways before crossing, never trusting me.

Occasionally he would be very late and appear walking, pushing the machine alongside.

'The chain's off again,' he would say, as he came closer. Then we both pushed the bike over the lines where he hopped on sidesaddle to freewheel down to the beach path.

The Hallion was a tough bike, but its one weakness was that the chain was always coming off. It had to be fixed and since we couldn't afford the local garage, my father would have to do it himself. Just about anything to do with tools put him in a bad temper. He usually set aside Saturday mornings for repairs and he would begin by opening the coal-shed door and wheeling out the Hallion. Then he would rummage for a screwdriver on the tool bench. When he had found one, he would look at the jagged edge, and, before he could blame me, I would vanish round the corner of the house. Next, he would light a Woodbine, in the process losing the tool. Then finding it again, as the cigarette at the corner of his mouth streamed smoke into his eyes, he would begin work. I watched as, once again, he would wrench off the chain case. Meanwhile, the heated fag-end would burn his lip and he would frantically try to spit it out till the torn cigarette butt lay smouldering on the damp ground. Some paper was still sticking to his lip. My mother would usually come out and take in the situation at a glance.

On Saturday, my friend Bert's father, Robert, sometimes walked his dog on the shore and, if so, Mother would intercept him. He was a bull of a man, with crinkly hair and jam-jar-thick glasses. She would invite him in, put a blue and white mug of tea in his hand, together with a large stick of shortbread, and then he would step into the yard.

'Trouble with the bike, Tam?' he would ask levelly and when my father replied, Robert nodded, and chewing the shortbread, slowly approached the bike. He would touch the sprocket as if it were injured, his eyes softening behind his thick glasses. Gently rocking the sprocket between his fingers, he would straighten up and, drawing a Capstan Full-Strength from his pocket, light it and consider the job.

Eventually his eyes would wander to the bench of ruined tools and he would set his cigarette absent-mindedly on one side. With a few tools and ever so gently he would soon have the problem solved. Finally, in silence, he would screw the chain casing on again, shaking his head sadly at the state of the screw heads. As he rose, he rubbed his head like a puzzled giant.

'That should be all right now, Tam,' he said refusing a half-crown from my father's hand.

'How's the writing? I read that piece of yours in the *Tellie* – about the Three Arches river. My father had told me some of that.'

Because most of his writing appeared in the *Belfast Telegraph*, recognition came from locals – the postman, the breadman, the guard on the train and neighbours. Father lived for writing and, although he did not respect bench tools, he had an affection – a love, even – for his pen. It was a black Parker 51 with a top made of silver whose clip was formed like a feathered arrow. He always wrote leaning on a piece of board which he'd fashioned from softwood found on the beach. At the top, holding the writing paper in place, was a large metal Bulldog clip. In the evenings after tea, he would settle in his armchair in the corner beside the bookcase and begin writing on his knee.

I would often be playing on the floor with a Meccano set, bolting together green and red metal pieces to make models. Up on a shelf the wireless would be playing softly, while below Mother read or knitted. From the corner came the scratch, scratch of the Parker 51 on paper. Before long I would hear his breathing getting laboured.

'Tom, you're holding your breath,' Mother would remark and then his breathing would quieten again. Eventually the scratching would slowly draw to a halt and Father would put the top on his pen, turn up the wireless for the nine o'clock news and ask when supper would be ready.

Quite a lot of his writing was about local folklore and he gathered material by talking with almost anyone who had a story to tell. At times he took the Hallion up into the Glens of Antrim to hear stories, for at that time there were even one or two native Irish speakers living there.

Mostly I was not allowed on these excursions but one Sunday morning I heard the engine of the Hallion echoing in the yard. As I opened the door to see what was going on, he waved me over.

'Do you want to come?' he shouted over the noise of the engine. Delighted to miss serving my church sentence, I nodded and ran ahead to open the railway gate and wave him up from the beach. Then I climbed on the back and we rode up into the hills. Beyond Glenariff, we turned into a lane, along the edges of which I noticed painted stones. We arrived in a small farmyard and stopped outside a newly whitewashed cottage. When Father cut the engine, my ears felt peculiar in the total silence. I looked around the yard which had boulders with odd, coloured markings painted on them.

The top half of the front door opened and an old farmer, unshaven and wearing a dirty, collarless shirt, leant over.

'Hello, Tom,' he called, 'and who might this young man be?'

Father did not reply and the farmer looked at us; I noticed that one of his eyes did not move.

'Come on in, the pair of you,' he said, opening the bottom of the half-door. As we went into the kitchen, I noticed that Father was carrying a big brown book.

'There's something I'd like to show you, Jimmy,' he said, opening the tome.

'Look, here's a Buddhist Mandala, like that boulder you have at the gate,' he said, leaning over, showing the page to the farmer, who lifted his cap and was scratching his head. I put on my interested face.

'Boodhism, you say — what would I want with the like of that? Aren't we all good Christian folk here?'

'We all worship the same God, Jimmy. There's some force working through all of us – through you, to make those pictures.'

'Ah, they just come on me some days.'

The farmer caught my eye. People who listened to my father's homilies would eventually meet my eye. After briefly holding the look to show understanding, I would look away again.

ON SATURDAY mornings I always walked into town. After climbing the lane up to Eden, I took the main road, passing the brick detached houses with thick gateposts which lined the route. I would look in at their blank, blind windows, thinking that the nameless inhabitants must be in there somewhere.

It was downhill all the way to Carrickfergus Castle and then into the town where I turned up North Street and into the pet shop.

'A quarter stone of maple peas, please,' I would say to Mr Hamilton over the noise of chirruping budgerigars. Two shillings – that was most of my pocket money gone. Only sixpence left.

When I had my first two baby pigeons, I had needed rings for their legs and Patsy, a small grocer and pigeon-fancier, had promised to get them for me. But weeks passed and they still hadn't turned up. I would have to go up to his shop and ask again. As I passed the church, I looked up at his huge loft which he shared with another pigeon fancier, Flutter. I opened the red door of the tiny grocery shop beneath and went in.

Inside it was dark and there was only room for four at most. Patsy was a short, pudgy-faced man with black hair. Elbows on the short counter, he was talking in his usual conspiratorial way with Flutter and Tappytoes.

I put my brown paper bag of maple peas on the counter. Patsy paused. 'Is that Special Mix? I always give mine Special,' he pronounced.

'Maple peas,' I said.

'Now, I wouldn't feed the birds maple peas. They'll run to fat,' said Flutter, a small, dark, thickset man with oily hair whose nickname came from his love of horseracing.

'But it's not as bad as crack corn,' said Tappytoes, looking down from his six-foot advantage. My father had told me that Tappytoes' nickname had nothing to do with dancing, but the fact that he had a French name, Taputeau, which locally became Tappytoes.

An old woman came in the shop; we fell silent.

'A packet of tea and a pound of sugar, Patsy. And five Woodbine. How's your mother keepin?' She counted out the coins, squinting in the half-light.

'Ah, she's a bit better, Cissy,' said Patsy scooping up the change. We all stood in total silence, waiting. I thought the customer must feel unwelcome.

'Well, I suppose you want to get back to your pigeon talk,' she said and left.

'Have you those rings yet?' I ventured. Patsy dug his hand into his trousers pocket behind the counter and produced four of them by magic in the palm of his hand. They shone silver in the dark.

'How much?'

'A shilling for the four.'

'I've only sixpence.'

'Then take two and get the others next week.'

A scrabbling noise started up, from pigeons in a wicker hamper on the floor.

'Patsy, wait till you see this,' said Flutter, bending down and reaching in for a bird. Flutter held his bird up to catch the poor light coming from the small, low window.

'D'you remember that book I showed you that I got in Belfast – about eye sign. It says if your bird has eye sign, you've got a winner. It's science.'

'Eye sign! Pie in the sky sign,' snorted Tappytoes.

'You can laugh – it's in a book. Isn't it Patsy?'

Flutter held up the bird.

'Look at that eye, would you.' Patsy and I strained to see.

'Do you see it there? Eye sign!'

I couldn't see anything.

'Right enough,' said Patsy.

'Where is it? I can't see it,' I said, squinting.

'Now, it's not everyone can see it. You have to have the gift. Come here, closer.'

I peered at the eye of the bird.

'D'ye see it now?'

'See what?'

'The eye sign. Can't you see it?'

'Where?'

'Do you see that ring there, round the pupil. It has a sort of wee green glow. D'you see it?'

I saw nothing.

'I have to go home, Patsy. I'll be in for those other rings next week,' I said, and left.

AT TWELVE THIRTY I would catch the bus home and get off in Eden village at the Picnic Café stop. Nobody could remember there ever having been a café there but the bus conductors kept the café alive in our imaginations. Then I walked down the lane to arrive home in time for dinner.

On Saturdays Father finished work at midday and we all sat down to the main meal at one o'clock. There was a light festive air to this meal, which marked an end to the week's work. On his second mug of tea, instead of going next door, as he did in the evenings, my father would lean back in his chair. He would tell stories and sometimes become philosophical, often speaking of the supernatural and the immensity of the cosmos.

'Even if it's big, it must stop somewhere,' I remember saying once.

'It's not our place to ask those questions,' he replied, but I persisted.

'Well, you're as big as you're small,' said my father, using one of his favourite expressions, as if that settled the matter.

'What do you mean?'

'You're as far as you're near.' Father ended the exchange and, if it was winter, took his tea into the front room to read Madame Blavatsky on the spirit world.

On summer afternoons he hung the fishing nets up along the side of the bungalow like a curtain, to mend them. This put him in a good mood.

'You see, you have to cut the holes in the net even bigger before knitting them up,' he would say, reaching into the breast pocket of his tartan shirt to bring out a small pair of curved nail scissors. As he concentrated, delicately snipping away at the jagged hole in the net, his almost feminine touch always surprised me. I stood in silence except for the noise of drawn and knotted cord as, with the wooden needle, he rhythmically knitted new meshes into the big hole.

WHEN BERT AND I weren't out on the shore in summer, we spent time with our pigeons for school holidays were the racing season. My pigeon loft was a shed built from drift-wood: a deep barred veranda at the front held a white-domed water fountain. On its roof the birds landed so as to slip inside through the bobwires designed to let them enter but not leave.

Bert already had a shed that acted as a loft for his ten birds. One day we were watching his birds circling the area.

'Why don't we start a pigeon club?' he said, as his birds were banking to land on the roof. He let out a loud whistle with his tongue against his teeth. The birds landed on the house roof, then he rattled the tin of pigeon beans until the pigeons fluttered down on to the loft.

'Who'd we get?' I said.

'Well, there's you and me. We could ask Eddie.'

'Creighton! Why would we want him – he only has the one bird!'

It was true. He kept his one pigeon in a tea chest with a chicken-wire front.

'He has the lend of a basket for sending the birds off – and there's a phone near his house,' Bert said.

To say the phone was near Eddie's house was stretching a point and, anyway, most of the time it didn't work. But we had to have a phone, to find out what time the birds were being released to race home, so Eddie became club secretary.

Our first race was from Omagh. Soon after stretching on seven rubber racing rings we had got from Patsy, we used Eddie's basket to send the seven birds by rail to Omagh. Since we could not afford a pigeon timing clock, we agreed the first rubber ring back at Eddie's would win.

When it was about time to release the birds in Omagh, I cycled over to the Creighton house. It was raining. Eddie's mother opened the back door. Her son was at the table chewing a sandwich. The rain was drumming on the roof.

'Would you like a sugar sandwich?' she said. I shook my head.

'I phoned the stationmaster at Omagh. The birds are off – they'll be in around three. There's a tail wind,' said Eddie in between mouthfuls. 'The rain'll clear later on.'

When my first bird got back, I sprinted over to Eddie's. Bert was already there. His face said it all: Eddie had beaten both of us by half an hour. We were indignant and when our next race was also won by Eddie's bird, interest in the club waned and I started going to watch Patsy's pigeons racing back to Carrick from exotic-sounding places like Nantes in France and San Sebastian in northern Spain.

MY EARLIEST MEMORIES of summer holidays from Eden school were of playing on the Point. A sea wall, clad in stone, it sloped steeply from the rocks to a wall along the top which continued round the corner of the bay out of sight.

In summer, families down from Belfast stayed in the bun-galows and often one of the boys joined us. Bert and I and whoever else was there sat upon the slope. To the west across the bay we could see Carrick Castle and, beyond its harbour, the pencilled outlines of Belfast's shipyard cranes in the haze.

When it was high tide, a weed-heavy sea rose and fell in the cleft between shore and sea wall. Screaming gulls, moving easily above the surging tide, picked things from the surface debris. I always looked down to the base of the sea wall at the thick wooden posts; I loved their mossy green colour. Waves, breaking over the posts and flowing up the sea wall to our feet, swiftly drained back down. As the tide rose, only the tips of the green posts appeared between the waves.

As we waited for the tide to fall, we sat up on the slope of the Point in the sun, idly tossing stones at each other. When the water had receded, we would climb down to pick whelks off the rocks and hammer them open with a big stone. Then we tied them on to a piece of string weighted by a stone and lowered the bait into the water by the posts.

'Water's dead clear, so it is,' someone always said as we leaned over the sleepers and looked down into the depths, watching the fronds of seaweed swaying up towards us. When no crab appeared, we climbed back up the wall and whit-tled at pieces of wood. After a while we slid down the wall and had a look over the posts again. Someone usually had crab interested in the bait and would gently pull up a green butcher crab, still hanging on to the bait by one claw. When he (they were always male) was landed, we got him across the shoulders with thumb and forefinger and dropped him into a jam jar. The Belfast boys took crabs up the incline of the sea wall to the Letterbox, a deep crack in the sea wall, and dropped them in. There they would die from lack of water. They said crabs were evil and should suffer, and although Bert and I agreed, we always felt unsure about the Letterbox and talked of them dying inside this crab graveyard. We much preferred to smash them with our heel, as I did myself when they were entangled in the nets.

As the afternoon wore on and the tide paused farther out, we walked over the sands to the sandbank where here and there were small black holes for a cockabillion to suddenly scoot a jet of water up into the air. We used to dig with our hands for these shelled creatures (*pholas dactylus*), down and down till our fingers touched the edges of their shells, then, working our fingers around we got underneath and pulled them up. In appearance they were like a very large mussel but with a large penis-like organ sticking out at one end. It was through this that they shot a jet of water high above the surface of the sand. The 'cock' was supposed to be great bait, but in truth we never caught anything with this exotic lure. The other legendary bait was ragworm. When you dug them up, they looked extraordinary. Multicoloured, they writhed with their dozens of legs – exotic centipedes.

Line fishing was not our only way to catch fish for in the pools around the big sandbank we would 'tread' for flat-fish. When a flatfish betrayed its presence by a flurry of sand, we quietly waded after it, then when the moment was right, placed a bare foot on top of it, reached down and picked it up. I would bring some to Ma, who 'loved a bit of fish' and especially because it came from her favourite grandson.

AT LOW TIDE, Bert and I often went searching among the dark patches of weed-covered rocks for green butcher crabs. One of us would stop and stand behind a boulder, legs well apart and bending over. Our fingers felt among the weed for the edge; then we would slowly lever up the heavy stone and wait for the water to clear. As we waited, we could see the red anemones on the underneath; we called them bloodsuckers. Then we would peer down into the shallow water below. An eel might skitter about and then disappear. One of us would reach down and lift up a green crab. Claws wide, it would strain to bite. Then the boulder was released, splashing us both.

Soon we were searching farther afield for the brick-red edible crabs which we took home to boil. When I brought the first few home, Mother boiled them and after they had cooled, I watched, fascinated as Father took one crab, and placed it, with its back down, in his left hand. With the other he ripped out the underparts: claws and legs, all in one.

'Do you see these?' he said pointing to a row of grey fleshy bits. 'Dead men's fingers! They're poison.'

I pictured the fingers of drowned seamen, decaying on the sea floor.

'How do you open these things?' my mother said, vainly trying to twist a claw apart. Father went out to the yard and returned with the hammer. He laid it on the wooden table, then taking the claw from her, placed it on the wooden table and, seizing the hammer, hit the claw. It smashed and crab-meat flew up into his beard. He laughed, Mother picked meat out of his beard and tasted it. She declared it good and smiled. Each of us took turns with the hammer to crack open the claws. The legs were too skinny and had little meat: you had to suck them and, after a while, the table was strewn with smashed crab shell. In the middle lay the claw hammer. Mother cleared away all the debris, then washed the back shells in the sink to use later for ashtrays.

In years to come, usually at the weekend, the whole family went crabbing. We would cross the wet ribbed sand, my father striding ahead. Mother and I stayed well behind, looking after my little brother, Joss, who would splash his way slowly over gillets, stumbling on seaweed-covered bumps.

About a mile out, we would carefully negotiate slimy green stones and arrive at a long sandbank. Beyond it, in the water, was a field of seaweed, which we were to christen the Tangles. There Father would wade out in the water and, after depositing Joss on a large rock, Mother always went straight for the rocks in the shallows to begin searching for crabs. We had to keep an eye on Joss for he usually ran out into the water. He also had a strange habit of eating sand, but it seemed to do him no harm.

My mother was a fearless crabber. Sweeping the curtain of weed aside, she plunged her hand under the rock and pulled out any crab that was underneath.

I would start farther out, somewhere between Father in the deep water and Mother at the edge. I too would sweep weed aside and, feet astride, lift a boulder. When I had raised it up enough I would pause to peer into the settling dust. Then, if there was no crab, I released the boulder, which dropped in the water with a dull plop.

Occasionally I rose to gaze at the blinding glitter of afternoon sun off the sea. Out of the corner of my eye, I could see Mother's stout figure bent over, scouring under the weeds, around the edges of rocks. Occasionally she pulled crabs from crevices, leaving them on their backs on the sand. There they flailed, bubbling from the mouth, unable to turn over.

We got interested in lobsters by accident.

ON SUNDAYS, when the tide was far out, Father walked for miles alone with Natasha, our Russian wolfhound, along the beach. On one such day, coming home, he saw a gillet in the distance. He loved that word 'gillet' – one of those rivers in the sand where the ebb tide drains away. No local knew the word, but he used it with relish, as if it had a good taste. Once when he started following the gillet's edge towards the shore, he came upon a dark object. As he drew closer, he saw the blue-black shell of a huge lobster and, thinking it was dead, nudged the shell with his stick. The creature stirred, then reared, big claws up sweeping for a target. He had to use both hands to carry the lobster home because it kept thrashing its tail and trying to get at him with its claws.

Back in the bungalow I watched as my mother brought out weighing scales: it registered fourteen pounds: I stared down at the blue-black monster that could just fit, diagonally, in the big sink. Then I got Joss and lifted him up to have a look, but he took hold of one of the lobster's red feelers: the creature stirred. Mother screamed and pulled us away.

My parents hoisted the steel bath, half-full of water, on to the stove. When it boiled, my father picked up the big lobster with both hands and dropped it into the boiling water. I stood up on a chair to witness the last writhings as its legs crumpled in the steam. I thought of hell.

After half an hour, my mother lifted out the hot orange-red creature and put it on the draining board. When it was cool, Father wrenched off a single claw and poked out enough meat with a knitting needle to fill two of the three salad plates for tea. After we had eaten it for three days and could take no more, Sadie came on her bike and took the remains of the lobster meat in the handlebar basket back to Trooperslane. We kept the orange claws up on a shelf and when visitors came, the huge pincers were taken down and shown around, to gasps of admiration.

Father soon abandoned crabs in favour of lobsters and at the Tangles could be seen in white thigh-boots wading slowly along in deep water.

'He's only after lobsters,' Mother would say as we both watched his slow progress. I could imagine his big white feet raising clouds of dust underwater in the jungle of tangled weed. He would stop and peer down into the water, gently probing with his gaff. At times he would stand motionless, then turn and silently raise his hand. At such times my job was to walk back on to the sand to fetch the wire fireguard. We would need this to block a lobster's escape route. I would wade out deep, water edging up my bare thighs. By the time I had passed the fireguard to him, the water would be near my waist.

Father would lower the wire wall softly into the water, then tell me to hold it steady. He would peer down into the murky water while probing with the gaff. Suddenly there would be turbulence in the water and we would glimpse a lobster's tail as it escaped out to sea. To my surprise, instead of blaming it on me, Father would say nothing but look cross, while I imagined it shooting tail-first, claws trailing behind, out into deep water. When I got back to where Mother was searching, she would hear my splashing.

'I suppose it got away,' she would say without looking up. I did not reply.

Squelching home, carrying two or three crabs, I would often walk on ahead. Sometimes I would look back at my tall father and stocky mother. My father strode ahead. He had caught nothing for there were very few lobsters in the Tangles. In later life I often thought of the painting of Don Quixote and Sancho Panza by Daumier: Don Quixote was tall and erect in the saddle, ready to charge windmills; his ever practical, stout companion, Sancho Panza, sat on a donkey by his side.

BY THE TIME Joss started at Eden school Mother had already begun working part-time in a Carrick sweet shop and she was often there in the evenings. Behind the high, glass counter, lost in a reading reverie, she would come to when she heard the loud ping of the shop bell and be ready for any customer. Sometimes I called in; it was strange talking to her in the quiet shop away from home.

My mother had always gone to the local library and brought back books for us all, especially Father. I was often with her in the morning waiting for the library to open. When Miss Blair, the librarian, arrived, she would unlock the door, go inside and lock it again while she prepared herself for the day's work. Eventually she retired and when the post of town librarian was advertised, my mother applied. During the interview, which was held in the Town Hall, she was asked the names of the authors of three books: *The Cruel*

Sea, *The Sea Around Us* and *Erewhon* – the first two of which she knew and the third, by Samuel Butler, she did not. When she got back home from the interview, she said that she was sure that she had got the job. Two weeks later she got a letter informing her that her application had been unsuccessful, so, disappointed, she stoically kept on working at the sweet shop.

One evening when she was reading her book behind the counter, the bell pinged. Mr Bell, one of the interviewers for the library job, walked in and asked for some bulls' eyes. She took the opportunity of asking him if it had been her lack of qualifications that had been held against her for the job. Mr Bell did not reply, but as he turned to go, he winked. A week later Mother discovered that the post was still unfilled and she was asked if she would like to work at the library part-time.

MOTHER'S JOB at the library coincided with my passing the Eleven-Plus exam when I was accepted into Ardilea House, the local branch of Belfast High School. There, for the first time in my life, I had to wear the uniform of blazer, tie, and grey flannel shorts. Bert, who had not sat the exam, was quite content to stay on at Eden Primary.

My new school was in an old country house, in its own grounds, six miles from home. I took the Belfast bus there each morning. Two teachers dominated my mind at that time: the headmaster, Mr Towell, nicknamed Humpy, and Mr Skingle. Humpy was a short, thick-set bachelor whose main interest in life was rugby and Jackie Kyle, its outstanding Irish player. I found the game fearsome and each Tuesday, practice day, I fervently prayed for rain. Humpy sometimes exceeded his authority and once declared that people who didn't play rugby would be failures in life. Incensed when she heard this, my mother wrote him a letter listing people like Churchill who, she said, had no time for the game. The problem really was that my father had been a well-known Carrick rugby player and I detested playing the game.

From his near seven-foot height Mr Skingle smiled calmly down on all of us, radiating benevolence. Each morning he arrived by bicycle and because of his great height, the effect was of huge stick insect, perched on a very small bicycle. What I liked about Mr Skingle most was that he treated us all equally. In class, he would quote bits from *Reader's Digest*, a magazine he held in high regard.

Then there was Mr Miles, the English teacher, who could not keep control of the class and often lost his temper. Once, in a rage, he had thrown an inkwell at a boy and cut his forehead. For some reason myself and Milesy, as he was called, liked each other. In retrospect, it may have been that he recognized our common lack of self-confidence.

Although I had several friends at Belfast High, these friendships did not extend beyond school hours and my life continued to be dominated by the village and its surroundings. Trevor, one of my new friends at school, came from Clipperstown, a Carrick suburb, and sometimes after school I went back to his house. There, in the quietness of the parlour, he would play the piano accordion for me. He tried to teach me, but I couldn't get the hang of the instrument. One day at break-time we spotted a new boy. His name was Sean and he came from the Free State. We knew this was a wicked place, although I didn't really know why. Neither Trevor nor I had ever been in the Free State and no one we knew had even expressed a wish to go there.

Oddly, I had forgotten that my father went down to Dublin from time to time to do programmes for Radio Athlone. If anyone left Eden or Carrick, it was usually to go to the so-called 'mainland' – England, for work. Every time Big Ben rang out for the BBC news, we were reminded that we were British.

Soon the word spread that the new boy, could speak something called 'Irish'. We all gathered round Sean one day and pleaded with him to say some words because we were amazed that there really was language called Irish.

'It's everywhere,' he said. 'The Rinka, that shop down Islandmagee – *rince* is Irish for dance.'

'It's just called that, so it is!' one boy retorted, seemingly offended at Sean's explanation. Later I got talking to Sean and asked him what it was like in the Free State and what was so bad about it. He replied that there was nothing wrong with it but that we, in Ulster, all thought it was a bad place because of the Rising. There was a new word for me. I must have looked puzzled and he asked if I'd never heard of 'the Troubles'. There it was: that word again. I thought of Pa.

'What was the Troubles, anyway?' I asked carelessly.

'Shooting,' said Sean. 'Catholics and Protestants shooting each other. It's all Protestants up here; they wanted to stay with the British. They brought guns in at Larne, the Irish Volunteers did. Then the South copied them.'

When I asked him how he knew all this, he told me his father was always talking about Irish history. I didn't like history much, although my mother had tried to help me with dates. 'In fourteen hundred and ninety-two Columbus sailed the ocean blue,' she would intone, but there was no such easy trick to remember that the battle of Bosworth Field was in

1485. Where was this field, anyway, and what was Bosworth doing there? For that matter who was Bosworth?

I realized later that this was the origin of my distaste for history: it was never about Ireland but about England's kings and queens. Father, on the other hand, although he never spoke of the Troubles, was a mine of information on Ulster folk tales. He had also written about the subject and some of his articles in the *Belfast Telegraph* were illustrated by the Belfast artist, Raymond Piper, who often visited us on the beach. In his suede shoes, what were then called chukka boots, he seemed very exotic to me. He sometimes visited when Father was away at work and would sit with my mother in the porch looking out over the lough. The two of them looked so happy together, but I never heard what they talked about.

Around that time I decided that I wanted to be an artist like Raymond Piper, but my drawings did not look right. I couldn't understand how some of the other pupils had found out how to draw and paint. I thought they must have been born that way, like having red hair or something.

I drew only German soldiers. I had found a piece of paper left on the windowsill at school, with an ink drawing of two German soldiers crouched behind a machine gun, one firing and the other feeding the belt of bullets into the weapon. I was gripped by the drawing and started copying it in class. Word got back to the young artist, fellow pupil Martin Majury, and soon drawings began to be left, as if by accident, on the windowsill. Martin was tanned, athletic and had blond hair. His father, who ran a shoe shop in Belfast, was rumoured to have been a German soldier.

The next drawings he left were SS officers, stern and unremitting. They always wore monocles. I had only seen a monocle once, when Father found his own in an old tin box from the war. He had his back to me at the time and, screwing it on to his eye, had turned round, giving me a terrible shock.

But my own drawings did not flow; the angular Germans I drew looked like alien robots with piercing eyes. Mother felt uncomfortable about them and drew some cheery RAF officers with handlebar moustaches for me to copy, but I had no interest in them.

I really liked the art teacher but she came to the school only once a week. From the class window I often watched her walking up the winding school avenue beneath the spreading trees. Miss Whitsitt walked with a rangy step and looked about her at the trees and the sky with an open joy.

One day she caught me drawing my Germans in her class. I tried to hide them, but she persuaded me to show them to her. I watched her face as she looked at them.

'Mmm … interesting … unusual…' her voice said, but her face looked troubled. Later in the class I caught her looking at me with a worried expression.

I seemed to have more ability in English class. Even though Milesy never could control the class, I came to appreciate that he had a real love of his subject. I had once written a story about a highwayman which he praised in class.

'Did you write this yourself?' he asked. I was so surprised that I could say nothing. The class moved in on me. 'Did you write that yourself? Did you write it yourself?' they mocked. It went on and on and Milesy could not control them. In desperation, I had to shout that I had got it from a book. Then they went quiet.

'We knew that. You couldn't have done it yourself,' they jeered in a kind of jagged chorus.

I think he suspected I had lied under pressure and that I had truly written it myself. Since that day, he was friendly to me.

My grades worsened at Ardilea. At Eden school, Mother had helped with homework, but now she was increasingly consumed by her interest in the library. School reports always arrived on a Saturday. I thought it must be to inflict the maximum misery on the victim, for these reports brought out the very worst in my father.

'Listen to this. Isn't this great? "Could do better",' he said sarcastically, '"Does not try; could do much better."' Even Humpy's enthusiastic: 'Has great potential but seems preoccupied' drew only the remark: 'Vacancy within – please apply.'

Many years later Aunt Sadie was a passenger in a car driven by my old science teacher, Miss Smith.

'By the way, what happened to your nephew, Ross?' Miss Smith suddenly asked.

'Oh, Ross is lecturing at Trinity College in Dublin now,' Sadie said airily. Shaken, Miss Smith took her hands off the steering wheel and the car nearly left the road. Sadie clearly enjoyed telling this story for she always related it with enormous relish.

What worried my parents was that I seldom read books and kept to Superman and horror comics. There was one story in particular which I never forgot. A girl from an orphanage is adopted by a rich couple, who appear to be charming and good people. However, at home in the mansion she is put to work as a servant and is beaten. She becomes despairing, frantic to please and so to avoid punishment. One day, resolved to clean the bathroom really well, she uses acid but accidentally leaves the bath half-full of the cleaning solvent. Her stepfather, not knowing this, jumps into the bath. Horrible screams are heard through the door as his body is consumed with acid. In the last frame of the comic strip, the girl is standing outside the door saying: 'I was only trying to get the bath *really* clean!'

MY UNHAPPY RELATIONSHIP with my father seemed to have had no beginning and no hope of ever changing. The most disturbing thing for me was that without warning he could suddenly heap praise on me for what I thought was not worth anything. One day at tea I was quiet during the meal and then he challenged me.

I replied: 'I have nothing to say.'

'By God, that's marvellous. The boy knows something,' he said, beaming at my mother. 'He who speaks does not know – he who knows does not speak.'

Meanwhile, Mr Skingle, so long the antithesis of Father, was to undergo a change in my eyes. One morning, it was snowing heavily. A snowfight had started at the school. Spirits were high and snowballs were whizzing in all directions amidst much laughter.

Through a gap in the merriment, I watched him ride up the avenue on his high bicycle, grinning as he surveyed the rowdy, snowballing teenage boys and girls. Suddenly a snowball hit him hard on the side of the head. The bike wobbled and he fell in the snow. I held my breath. Mr Skingle stood up, brushing the snow off his clothes. The kindly smile had vanished. Face contorted, he snarled at the offender to come forward. The snow was falling thicker now, and, raising his angry voice into the storm of flakes, he announced to us that the whole school would stay in an extra hour till five. That day his mask had slipped; underneath he was not so different from Father.

IN SCHOOL one day I counted nearly a hundred bikes. At lunchtimes, I used to pore over the gears, rims and frames of the exotic machines: Mapplebeck, Claud Butler and a much-admired Andre Bertin, named after the French cycling champion. Sometimes I looked in awe at Mr Skingle's bike. Being so tall and riding a normal size bike might have presented a problem for him but he had remedied this by having a one-foot seat extension welded on and also a handlebar extension. To make the bars even higher, he had turned the drop handlebars upwards, steer-like.

I badly wanted a bike but all my pocket money went on pigeon beans. My parents could only just afford the half a crown each week and so I did not mention it, but I did tell Bert.

'Build one yourself,' he said.

'Can you do that?'

'Paul McCullough did.'

The next day we went round to Paul's house in smoky West Street, Paul opened the door. He was short and tubby; behind him stretched a long bright corridor. In it stood the bike, its royal blue and chrome frame reflecting the light.

'Did you make it all yourself?' I asked in disbelief, leaning over the frame and admiring the derailleur gears.

'Except the wheels,' said Paul. 'My uncle bought them for me.'

In that moment, I decided to make my own bike; I would worry about the wheels later.

I took to staring in the window of Pierce's bicycle shop in Carrick and before long I was invited in to chat with the shopkeeper who always spoke though his large nose. Mr Pierce allowed me to hang around in his shop. When I looked up, above my head was a forest of new tyres hung from the rafters. New bikes were parked diagonally at the front of the shop, but the workshop in the back was fascinating.

On the bench rested the bike currently under surgery. It was surrounded by sprockets and chains, all hanging on the walls, along with rims and hubs, cables and levers. On one wall was a poster showing a black youth riding his Raleigh bike, laughing as he is pursued by a lion. The other wall had a poster of Reg Harris, the then world sprint champion, with his improbably pink cheeks, standing in a field, holding a red Raleigh track bike.

To build a bike, the first thing was to find a frame and it had to cost nothing. I had no idea where to get one, but one day Bert and I were searching for trout in the Copeland river. We were wading upriver, under the railway bridge, into what we called the Jungle: a patch of land beside the river, covered by big broad-leaved plants. Since they were shoulder high to us, the huge leaves formed a canopy under which we could play. Unobserved, giggling and whispering, we used to watch passersby on the back lane. Occasionally our quarry, as if by a sixth sense, would hesitate, look around and sniff the air like an animal. Then, thinking they must have been mistaken, they would go on their way. This sent us into convulsions. Don, the madman from the farm, did not usually venture down as far as the Jungle so we didn't have to worry about him.

On this particular afternoon we found a deaf and dumb couple picking blackberries from huge briars. They ignored us, working away in harmonious silence, often using a walking stick to hook down the high branches. They had one bucket already full. Bert and I were running through the Jungle when I tripped over something hard and angular. To inspect the object, we tugged it out from beside the remains of a dead rat: it was a bicycle frame. It didn't look too bad; it wasn't bent but Bert remarked on the rust.

I wasn't listening. It wasn't bent: I had my frame! As I carried it along the back lane, the deaf and dumb man stopped picking and came over. We stopped, he put down a half-full bucket of blackberries and silently inspected the rusty frame. With his fingertips, he touched under the cross bar where the metal was rippled. He signed something to his wife who looked worried. Then he pointed at the ripples again and, looking into our faces, shook his head.

For the next week, doubts put aside, I rubbed and rubbed the frame with old emery cloth before painting it green. It was this frame or nothing. Sometimes Mr Pierce let me rummage through the junk box and salvage parts. By feeding the pigeons the cheapest food, crack corn and sometimes bread, I managed to save enough for a set of gears. The shop-keeper bought me a Simplex derailleur gear down from Belfast and soon the bike was almost complete – except for one thing: the wheels. I just could not afford them.

Then I had a thought: if I could make a bike why not make the wheels too? I would copy an old wheel. Over the next weeks I found two wheel rims and Mr Pierce gave me two old hubs. The only expense was the spokes which he got me from Belfast, as well as a spoke key for tightening them.

One Saturday morning I began to build a wheel out on the bench in the yard, copying the lacing of the spokes of an old wheel. My father passed by.

'What are you at now?'

'Building a wheel.'

'What for?'

'I'm making a bike.'

'Oh,' he said and walked off, dragging the heels of his white waders on his way down to the beach.

By lunchtime I had one wheel made but when I spun it, it was badly buckled. After lunch I made the other one; the nipple key for the spokes grew hot in my hand, but that wheel wouldn't come straight either. By dusk I was still working at the bench. I could hardly see the spokes now and was close to despair. Without warning, our neighbour Jack's head popped over the fence.

'What are you at, Ross?'

'I'm trying to get this wheel straight,' I replied, near to tears. Jack was quiet for a while, then spoke:

'I always find it's a good thing to sleep on problems. Call it a day and start again tomorrow.'

More because of Jack's calm tone than his words, I laid down my bits and pieces in the near dark and went inside. Father was reading and my mother was knitting. Neither of them mentioned the bike. The next morning I finished the wheels with ease; they weren't perfect, but they worked. Later, when Jack looked over the fence I grinned as I showed him.

Everyone was full of praise for my achievement: I cycled up to Trooperslane and Ma declared me a genius. The boys at school praised me behind my back.

'Not bad,' said my father.

There was one thing that upset me: Father would not let me build a shelter for the bike, but instead offered me the coal shed whose back was actually a hedge and where rain leaked down on the coal and coal dust. So I had to leave my bike against the back of the bungalow covered with bits of old tarpaulin. Every time I heard heavy rain pounding on the wooden roof, I stiffened, picturing the rust stains I would find on the handlebars in the morning. But for the most part I basked in glory for several months and went cycling in the Antrim hills.

One day I stopped for a rest at the top of a hill. I was eating my sandwiches when I heard the pounding of a Lambeg drum. Two people were climbing the hill. The big drum was being carried on the back of one man, while the other followed, beating the drum with small canes. As they came closer, I could see that the man carrying the drum on his shoulders was very thin, the expression on his face concentrated. The stout drummer, sweat pouring from his face, was in his shirt sleeves. As they approached, the stout man paused his beating and the thin man slowed. They halted beside me.

'Warm work!' said the big man.

'Aye,' said the drummer. The thin man helped him on with the big drum and they set off again this time, with the thin man keeping up the furious rhythmic blattering.

On the morning of the Twelfth of July my mother would call me and my brother outside to hear the beating of the Lambeg drums, echoing off Cave Hill, twelve miles away. Later in the morning Bert and I would go into Carrick to see the bands. We lined the shore road until the sound of the pipe band drifted towards us on the wind. Down the hill would come King William riding a white horse. Bewigged and sitting tall in the saddle, he would lead the Orange banners proudly into town, although everyone knew he was really Alec McQuitty, the milkman. Behind him came a forest of pipers, all in kilts, with the drum major at their head. As the pipers approached the town, the drum major threw his mace up high and caught it as he marched. We used to try this with the broom at home, but it sometimes gave you a bad crack on the skull when it came down.

On a stone step in the old harbour was the imprint of a horse's hoof. It was supposed to signify the fact that King Billy had landed in our town, but I didn't know why the shoe print was facing out to sea. My father always remarked that the king had taken one look at Carrick and decided to leave. He also told me that once, as a boy, he had cut through a Carrick Orange parade on his bike. Two Orangemen had drawn their swords and chased him all over town until he escaped through a hole in a hedge. They had reported him to his father, but Pa was not impressed – he had no time for Orangemen.

FATHER, having abandoned labouring some years earlier, was now storeman for the Electricity Board in Carrick. Although this job gave him the freedom and energy to write, he still did not seem to actually enjoy anything and was like a man with a perpetual toothache. His drift nets, far from being a pleasure, were a duty, and his writing, an essay in pain and rejection, put him in a bad temper. But by Saturday he would expand into storytelling over the midday meal. His gift for exaggeration and metaphor transcended the mundane little bungalow and he transformed the world into a poetic place. When it was raining and the roof leaked he could still work his magic whether talking of the war in Italy or retelling a local story.

The flat, wooden roof, which was covered in felt, was supposed to be tarred once a year. It was usually done with a bucket of tar and a long-handled brush, but my father, whose head was filled with ideas about the mystical oneness of the universe, would forget to do this, so that when we ate, we often had to suffer rainwater dripping on to the table. As soon as the dripping started, my mother would place a mug to catch the water. But then more drips came down somewhere else and got worse until she would put down a dish to catch the water. By the end of dinner there would be saucepans on the floor too. The din was loud and when Father's talk could no longer be heard, he would announce his intention of going outside to tar the roof. Inside, it sounded as if a giant was tramping around up there for he wore his white wader boots to do the job.

Several years of writing had yielded only a few broadcasts and articles published in the *Manchester Guardian* and the Ulster newspapers. Mother, determined to help, contacted Aunt Joyce in Plymouth. My aunt had worked for Lady Astor, the first British female Member of Parliament, who was related to the editor of *The Observer*. When six of Father's essays appeared in that paper, he must have felt he was at last getting somewhere and that if he wanted to be a bona fide writer, it was now or never. He then announced to my mother that he was going to write full-time and live from fishing. He turned a deaf ear to my mother's protestations.

'To hell with poverty!' he roared and laughed up at the wooden ceiling. Since he refused to take unemployment benefit, from then on we lived on my mother's scant earnings from the library, together with what he could earn from selling fish and the occasional article.

By winter 1955, whenever I came home from school, Father was always there, scratching away in the corner. He did not speak.

I would eat some left-over crusts from breakfast my mother would leave in the cold oven.

'We need wood for the fire,' would come his loud voice from the front room just as I was taking a drink of buttermilk.

'But the weather's terrible.'

'Men must work and women must weep.'

'In a minute then.'

'Now,' he would roar and I would take a sack and go out again to search for driftwood along the shore.

Mother, unhappy about his full-time writing, spoke less to him and at the silent mealtimes I kept my head down, occasionally glancing at the veins standing proud on the back of my father's hand. Out of the corner of my eye I would see Mother's quick, precise movements of knife and fork. Often a sound of scraping would start over in the kitchen cupboards. We would all pause, but as soon as we continued eating, the sound of a rat gnawing its way through the boards would become louder. I would stiffen and my father, irritated, would tell me to take care of it.

After tea I would search the cupboards for an old cocoa tin, but if there was none I would have to use the new one. Emptying the remains of the current tin into a spare cup, I would pull it apart to form a square metal plate. Then, taking a torch, I would open the floor cupboard door and go in on all fours to find the new rat hole. After cutting the cocoa tin material to size with a pair of scissors, I nailed on the patch so that the rats could not eat their way through. Even with the torch and the tin shining in the dark, I could hardly see and often hit my fingers with the hammer.

When spring came the net was put out and we caught grey mullet and even some salmon each week. My mother would take any salmon into Carrick and sell them in Hilditch's fish shop, but if the fish had been mauled by a seal or crabs we would eat it ourselves and often had salmon salad. Mullet would not sell so we often had it for dinner. By far the most common catch was dogfish – the cheapest option in fish and chip shops where it was usually sold as 'rock salmon'. We threw them back in the sea, but they usually swam right back into the net again.

Towards the end of that summer the weather began to deteriorate and one morning I woke to the sound of rain drumming on the wooden roof as gale force winds buffeted the walls of the bungalow and it felt as if we would be lifted off the ground. It was impossible to see out of the windows because water was flowing down the glass and by late morning Mother had put old coats at the bottom of the doors to keep out the rain. Still at lunchtime the roof leaked on to the table and so we ate with various saucepans and containers catching the drips.

In the afternoon, when the storm had abated, we got ready to go out to the net at low tide. The sky was still overcast and there was a cold wind. We stumbled over broken branches of tangle weed and finally reached the net curving out from the Point across the stormy bay. As we got closer, a shocking sight slowly revealed itself: the net was now rolled into a thick brown rope containing fish, crabs, weed, and rocks from the storm. I was taken aback. Father's bearded face was set hard and he did not speak.

Normally the net hung like a curtain in the water, the head rope buoying it up with corks and the bottom rope pulling it down with lead weights. In the storm, the bottom rope had been swept over the top rope, again and again, forming a

200-yard, ragged bulging sausage filled with debris. We tried to unravel it, but it was hopeless. The pain of freezing hands was terrible and when they grew even colder, I told my father.

'Keep on going; they'll warm up,' he said, and even as he spoke I noticed they were warming slightly. In ten minutes they began to glow.

After an hour of disentangling barnacle-covered rocks, tins, crabs and weed from the meshes, my father stopped. We had done only six yards in the hour, so he sent me home for the wheelbarrow. When I got back, he had taken his penknife and sawn through the net in three places cutting it into four pieces. We made several journeys back to the house with him wheeling and me holding the net on the barrow. But when part of the net was cleaned it was clear it was too badly holed to be any use and so we were now without a net.

Luckily we still had the old net, but it mostly caught grey mullet which we now ate several times a week. I began to dread evening meals and the inevitable fish. One evening I simply could not eat it again and I sat looking at my plate.

'Eat up, boy,' my father snapped.

'Tom, even the dogs won't eat it any more,' Mother said. He grunted.

Occasionally she went to the butcher's in Carrick and after buying a few meagre chops would ask for 'some meat for the dogs'. One day she told me she had been on the way home on the train from shopping in Carrick. She had two parcels from the butcher and she opened them on her lap. With a shock she realized that the dog meat was better than our own and from then on we ate the dog meat. I assume the butcher had taken pity on us and it was his way of helping us out of very hard times without embarrassing my mother.

FOR A LONG TIME NOW, there had been ancient gunpowder flasks hanging on the wall beneath an old muzzle-loader rifle. I noticed they had gone and when I asked Mother, she admitted they had been sold, along with all the silver fish knives and forks. I knew now that things were bad.

My mother confessed to me years later that during this time she had bought a pair of fine court shoes out of the grocery money, even though she knew the stones on the lane would ruin them in weeks. She had felt the need to buy them to help save her sanity. Sometimes she leafed through the Houses for Sale section in old copies of *Country Life*, dreaming, no doubt, of what might have been. Christmas of 1952 was particularly bleak since we could afford only a chicken and Mother warned me beforehand that my present would have to be my new school blazer.

While Mother cooked the chicken, Father, as was his custom, went into Carrick to find anyone in the streets who might be alone for Christmas. That year he returned with a small, thin, balding man called Joe, who had previously come for Sunday dinner more than once. A mild-mannered man, he had a reputation for getting blind drunk and taking his Lambeg drum out into the streets at night, wakening the town. He was also a man of few words and on his Sunday visits to our house would refuse a drink, then sit in silence waiting for dinner to be ready. At the table Father would always break the silence with the same question: 'Have you seen Aikie lately, Joe?'

'I hain't seen Aikie this long while, Tom.'

And that was the extent of their dialogue.

But this Christmas was to be different because Joe was drinking again and, after a couple of whiskeys, he started talking about an earlier festive season when a local girl had been murdered just five miles up the road at Whiteabbey.

Patricia Curran, a nineteen-year-old judge's daughter, had been discovered by her brother, Desmond, on the avenue up to their large house. She had been stabbed thirty-seven times. By the time I got to school the following morning, everyone knew. It was a huge shock for adults and children alike. The impact seemed greater because it was the daughter of such a 'high up' person. In class, Mr Wylie had simply remarked to us that it was obvious 'some poor fellow couldn't take it' and I think we all assumed it was a criminal's revenge. The story was carried in the *Belfast Telegraph* every day for months. When Ian Gordon, a young RAF man stationed nearby, was charged with the murder and declared guilty but insane, the fuss and drama died down. I remember Mother acidly remark that the victim's brother, Desmond, had been spirited away to Africa.

Apparently Joe's sister, Flo, a nurse at the mental hospital where Gordon was committed, had told him that he was treated more like a guest than an inmate and was not pre-scribed any medication.

'I told you, Tom: that man was never insane,' Mother pro-nounced as she tore off some chicken flesh from the carcass.

Years after that, it emerged that Gordon had been sub-jected to a gruelling interrogation and forced to make a statement describing how he had stabbed Patricia Curran to death. Although he was soon a free man, it took him fifty years to clear his name.

AFTER CHRISTMAS it was back to a diet of fish but if we were to survive and eat anything different from grey mullet, it was going to be essential to use the longline.

'Dig some bait in the morning, boy,' Father would say the night before we went fishing. I would then spend the whole of Saturday morning digging bait on the sand and threading worms on hooks. It was a messy business – doubling the head of the worm back and forth on to the barb and nipping off the sand-filled tail. The spilt worm guts always left brown stains like iodine on your hands. When I was done, the whole baited line lay on a wooden tray, some one hundred baited hooks lying in rows.

When Father crunched down the shingle from the bungalow in his white wader boots, I would be ready at the oars. As he pushed out the boat, its keel grating on the stones, he hopped in. The weight pushed the small boat down into the water, alarmingly.

'Pull! Pull! Put your back into it!' he would shout from the stern, the longline tray before him.

'Keep the bungalow behind my head at all times,' he would say as I hauled on the creaking oars, adjusting direction as required by rowing stronger on the right or left oar. I kept the bungalow blotted out behind his choleric, bearded face.

After twenty minutes or so rowing straight out to sea, he would call a halt and I rested on the oars. We did not speak and the boat rose and fell with the slight swell as he checked the long line.

'Run slowly before the tide while I pay out the line. Keep your hands on the oars.'

I would pull with one oar and push with the other, manoeuvering the boat into position. Then, as we ran before the tide, he would pay out the long line from the stern while I braked gently with the oars. It usually went smoothly but when a few hooks caught together, I would have to brake sharply and back-pedal with the oars. This allowed my now irritated father to disentangle the bloody, baited clump. If he could not untangle it, he would give up, curse and let it go.

Once we were paying out the line and as the boat ran faster before the tide, a big bunch of hooks lifted off the tray. He made a grab for it and I braked, but too late and the hooks caught his hand.

'Back up! Back up!'

When the line was finally paid out and the end marked by a floating paint can, tied to the line, I rested on the oars, dipped in the green water. There was a mild swell and the boat would rise high and fall slowly with a pleasing rhythm. Father would light a Wild Woodbine from a pack of five and inhale deeply as he stared out over the water at the green, County Down coast. At these times I stole a glance at the man who scared me all the time – his weather-beaten face was at peace. He was calm; both of us silent, the only sound the creak of the rowlocks.

'We could have a look now,' he would suddenly announce, calmly tossing his cigarette butt into the water. Then I rowed us back to the floating paint tin and my father caught the line beneath it with the boat hook. Hand over careful hand, he would pull the boat along the line. From my place at the oars I watched hooked fish swaying their way to the surface. When the big codfish reached the surface, they looked such monsters – with their strange colours and bulging eyes, they could have come from another planet. He would take each one off and drop it into the bottom of the boat.

On one of these occasions, when we were finishing, the green sea had turned to a choppy brown.

'Pull harder!' he barked, looking at the clouds overhead. 'Keep that steeple behind me.' He pointed at the Down coast but I could hardly see it now because it was blurred by rain. My arms ached with the strain of keeping the stern in line with the church across the lough. It was difficult, for the sea was pushing us off course all the time. The pain was getting really bad. I was weakening and the sea started coming over the side of the boat.

Father did not lose a moment; he pulled out the spare oars from under me, hastily inserted another pair of rowlocks and sat in front of me. By now the boat was rocking dangerously, but when his short powerful strokes began, it pulled us round on course again.

When we finally came ashore, the keel bouncing off the rocks, Mother was there waiting for us.

'Are you all right?' she said, wringing her hands in her apron. Father handed her a bucket of codfish.

'Just a bit of a wind,' he said offhandedly but I knew: I had seen the fear on his face out on the water.

AT THE END of the year, Father was still publishing sporadically in *Country Life* and the *Anglers Times,* but there was no breakthrough nor even the hope of one and he was becoming dispirited.

Seeing Father's spirits sink lower and lower, Mother became desperate to cheer him up and one day she saw an advertisment for Mensa – an organization for those with a very high IQ.

She sent away for an application without telling him, but giving his name and address. When the letter arrived he was thrilled and felt recognition had come his way from an unexpected quarter. That evening he opened the test forms on the kitchen table and he tried as many of the questions as he could. When it was done, he came into the front room and sat back puffing on the curly pipe which nestled in his beard. The next day Mother posted it into the red letter box in Eden.

The reply from Mensa was a long time coming but it finally arrived on a Saturday morning. He had been at work and when he got home at lunchtime it was sitting by his plate. Without waiting to change out of his work-clothes and wash, he tore open the envelope. Then he left the room, leaving it open on his plate. Mother picked it up. Her face fell: he had not been invited to join Mensa. When he returned, she confessed that it had been her idea to contact them; we ate lunch in silence.

On Sunday morning I saw him preparing a sandwich, then he went out the door putting the lunch package in his pocket.

'Where are you going?' my mother asked.

'For a bit of a walk,' he replied over his shoulder. 'Expect me when you see me.'

When he got back at dusk, he just said he had spent the day going round the cliffs at Islandmagee.

Three clothes parcels arrived in the post one day. Mother told us that they had come from Joyce Grenfell, the English actress with whom she had been in correspondence for several years. She told me that she had been so miserable that she had blurted out the state of our poverty in one of her letters and the parcels were the result. Many years later I was to be invited to lunch with Joyce Grenfell at her Chelsea home.

The clothes were almost all for men and my father now found he had more clothes than he knew what to do with. Two items took his fancy: a hard-wearing corduroy hacking jacket and a pair of plus fours. Sometimes on his lone weekend walks, he wore the plus fours with bright yellow socks.

'He has the leg for them,' my mother would declare to anyone who commented on his appearance. But she had her limits.

'Tom, you look ridiculous,' she snapped one day when he dug out his old monocle from a war box and screwed it into his left eye. He didn't wear it again.

We were finally saved by Mother becoming full-time town librarian for which she earned a modest salary. Although she did not have qualifications, she had become respected and indispensable to Carrick. At that time, all the men borrowed westerns and the women romances, and the 'serious' books were kept upstairs. Her first initiative was to transfer many of the upstairs books downstairs where they could be displayed and borrowed. She also encouraged workers to drop in wearing their overalls and advised parents on books to help their children with school.

Over tea she would regale us with tales from work, like the two women who would read books only about Eskimos or the man who always used a kipper as a bookmark. My father was not at all put out by her success and now cooked the evening meal, which, however, was usually burnt. He continued to write for some time, with mixed success, and although we still had little money, we were occasionally able to eat something other than fish.

ON SATURDAYS Father often went down Carrick Quay. One day, on his return I held the railway gate open for him. Instead of looking right and left, he rode straight across the railway line without his customary hesitation, before cruising downhill to the beach.

When Mother heard the engine being cut at the side of the house she came out, wiping flour from her hands on her apron. He took off his goggles and helmet; we saw he was smiling.

'Don't tell me there's good news?' she said, polishing her glasses on the apron. He didn't reply at first but put the goggles into the helmet and followed her inside. Sensing an occasion, she offered him tea and took down a large cup and saucer from the shelf. It was painted with mauve cockerels; Italian, she had bought the only one in the local hardware shop for him, and although he would not admit it, he treasured it.

Father hunched over the wooden kitchen table and put the heavy, chipped cup to his lips. We waited.

'I was talking to the Uncle Fred down the quay.'

Uncle Freddie, Pa's brother, had a droopy grey moustache, brown at the edges, which concealed his upper lip. Now nearly eighty, he always wore a blue pinstripe suit and waistcoat with a gold watchchain. He could be seen about the town, swinging his walking stick as he took the air. He was a slim, dapper figure and wore his hat at a rakish angle, which he always took off to the ladies he met.

'He still has that old motorboat, you know.'

'Oh, you mean *The Gannet*?' my mother said innocently.

'*The Puffin*,' corrected Father, 'he wants to lend it to me to do trawling.'

'Freddie never gave away anything for nothing.'

'I told him he could stay for a bit – he's on his own since Martha died.'

'What!' my mother said, going red.

'We could move Joss into Ross's room,' he said, 'and put them in bunks. Look – it's only for a while … returning a favour.'

'I am not moving them on any account.'

She got up and started peeling carrots into the sink. After a few minutes Father got up and went into the other room. She followed him in. I heard her raised voice.

Later, I was asking her if Uncle Freddie was really coming to stay when Father appeared.

'Yes, he is,' he said, ignoring Mother, who looked furious.

THE FOLLOWING WEEK there was more activity when Tony Cowan, my father's most constant friend, offered to tow *The Puffin* from the town. A big man in a donkey jacket, he had a large Roman nose and black curly hair. Tony and Father had a robust friendship, a typical exchange would go:

'Ah, Cowan, you Fenian bastard!'

Tony would grin and retort.

'Well, how's the bearded beast?'

My father would laugh with pleasure.

Tony's father had been an Italian Catholic but Tony had been reared in Antrim. His wife, Milly, was from Donegal and although Tony had a terrible temper, she seemed able to manage him, at least some of the time. Years later, she told me a trick she had for whenever he came in raving and ranting. She would tell him to sit down while she made him a cup of tea and then, in the privacy of the kitchen, she would put some Librium in his strong tea. Half an hour later he could not be more helpful.

The next weeks saw *The Puffin* eased down the slipway and sunk in the harbour. This would ensure that the parched boards could swell, closing up any gaps.

Two Saturdays later Father and I went to see the boat. A low tide had drained the harbour and *The Puffin* lay on her side in the mud. Freddie and I watched as Father, in waders, sloughed over the brown wasteland. On his way, he sank deeply but each time managed to extricate himself and struggle on until he reached the now wretched-looking craft. Then, using a rusty bucket, he bailed it out and later the three of us watched the boat lift with the incoming tide.

'She looks well. It does my heart good to see her afloat,' said Freddie, taking off his hat and putting it back on.

Meanwhile, the steel bunk beds had arrived and were left resting against the back of the bungalow. That evening, after our meal in the alcove, instead of retiring with his mug of tea, I watched my father gulp it down and go out to the yard.

By the time we had cleared the table, Father had returned with a hammer and a big screwdriver. He disappeared into Joss's room behind the alcove. Almost immediately came the sound of hammering and splintering wood.

Then we heard Joss crying and rushed to his room. My father was breaking up my little brother's large wooden cot. But it was the violence that struck me. Father seemed possessed and oblivious to Joss's screams. Then he paused and looked perplexed at my brother's tears.

'What's wrong with him?' he asked.

'You're smashing up his bed,' Mother said, 'he thinks he'll have nowhere to sleep.'

I bent down to comfort Joss.

'Don't worry, Joss, we'll be sharing bunk beds in my room. That'll be fun!'

Mother took Joss away while I carried out the pieces of the cot to the woodpile where their pale blue contrasted oddly with the brown coloured driftwood already piled up there.

The following weekend, Uncle Freddie arrived from Carrickfergus in a taxi with just a small suitcase. More of his belongings arrived early in the afternoon when a horse and cart came to the house piled high with hundreds of religious books. Then, at teatime, another cart arrived. Perched on top of this, upside down, was Pa's rowing boat, *The Canary*, which was then laid out on our small lawn. A hundred years old and split open at the bows, it had been down at the harbour since Pa's death. Freddie inspected it and got Father to turn it over.

There it lay on the grass, the two halves hanging apart at the bows while the two men gazed at it intently.

'Leave it to me,' said Freddie. 'We'll have that fixed in no time.'

My father didn't argue, for the old uncle had been a ship-wright in Carrick shipyard all his life. Within a few days, under Freddie's instruction, he had screwed the two halves of the bow together and, using a mixture of tar and cement, sealed up the big cracks from the inside of the old boat. Now, anyone looking into the rowing boat merely saw a thick crust of black sand.

'That's more like it,' Freddie pronounced, grinning at my father.

The day the boat was to be put in the water, all the beach residents appeared on the shore, probably expecting to watch *The Canary* sink.

'I'd say that's a Russian boat, Tom,' said Jack from next door. My father looked perplexed for he knew Pa had built her himself.

'What do you mean?'

'The water rushin' in and rushin' out of her,' he replied with a roar of laughter. But that day, and for two more years to come, *The Canary* floated gracefully on the water.

THE PUFFIN was moored fifty yards out from the bungalow and, from then on, our bay was dominated by the twenty-foot motorboat with three portholes. Newly painted red and white, I thought she looked splendid as she tugged gently at her rope with the rise and fall of the summer sea.

Now that we had a decent boat, my father thought every-thing would be all right. He could catch more fish and drop more lobster pots farther down the coast. The 'Ancient of Days', as my father insisted in calling Uncle Freddie (after Blake), was still settling in, although my mother did not know where to put all his assorted books. Some were packed into the already full outside lavatory. The remaining books ended up under a tarpaulin, weighed down by stones in the back yard.

Freddie also brought with him the Velocipede, a very early bicycle model, whose high wooden and iron wheels were just my height. He told us that as a young man he had often cycled to Belfast and back on what was then called the 'bone-shaker' – a round trip of twenty-four miles. It was put in the shed with no back wall and, although weathered by rain and wind, it was eventually donated to the Ulster Folk Museum.

WEEKS PASSED and Mother soon realized that five people rising in the morning at the same time was too much for the small bungalow. She decided to take Freddie his breakfast in bed each morning; then, after everyone else had gone, he could get up at his leisure.

This idea worked because the old man was little trouble and, after a long daily walk and his dinner, he sat quietly smoking his pipe in the evenings. He and I got on well as, unknown to my parents, Freddie slipped me half-crowns from time to time.

But soon, Mother began complaining that Uncle Freddie kept asking for extra things at breakfast. She seemed increasingly unhappy with the arrangement.

One morning Father was leaving for work when my mother, hot-faced and crying, rushed out of Freddie's room.

'Either he goes or I do. You can choose!'

'What's happened?' I said, open-mouthed.

'Disgusting old man!'

'I have to go. We'll talk later,' Father replied.

'No, now!' she insisted and they went out to the porch where I couldn't hear.

Two days later Freddie left. Uncle and nephew stood outside the bungalow in the morning sun; *The Puffin*, half full of water, was bobbing slowly before them on a glittering sea. The old man stood saying nothing, his cheeks flushed. Although my father was angry with his uncle, he did not speak and the two men watched the motorboat slowly orbit its mooring on the sandbank. My father, stiff with embarrassment, must have felt unequal to criticizing the 'Ancient of Days'. The tension was broken by the sound of a taxi crossing the railway line. It stopped and Father held the door open for Freddie to get in.

'You can have the boat,' said the old man just as my father was closing the rear door of the taxi that would take Freddie to his new lodgings. This was a house in Eden village which, surrounded as it was by a large orchard, was called 'The Garden of Eden'.

After Uncle Freddie left, Mother brightened for a while but she soon returned to worrying aloud about how to feed everyone. Father's response to poverty was to adopt a Great Dane and so we now had three dogs to feed, as well as four people. The new dog, Silva, had a huge scar in the middle of her back so that when we were out walking with the dogs, people saw the large, dark mark on the big dog, and looked accusingly at us.

Although Freddie's name was never mentioned, the boat was out in front of the house, to remind us of him every day.

Weeks passed as *The Puffin* sluggishly rode the waves at high tide. At low tide she lay tilted on a sandbank.

'When are you starting work on the boat?' I asked my father.

'Not yet, I've to get the timber,' he replied.

Eventually the wood arrived from Belfast and I watched, excited, as it was unloaded from the lorry and stacked outside the back door. Soon my father started to ask around for help in bringing the boat high up above the beach.

At this time we had a small pram dinghy: a tiny vessel, little more than a box with two square ends, on which, as a joke, my father had written 'the sharp end' and on the other, 'the blunt end'.

One evening he took the dinghy and rowed out to the motorboat. As he got ready to lever himself up to the bigger boat, a squall lifted her and he fell back into the dinghy, nearly sinking it. Forced to abandon attempts to board, he watched helplessly as the weather worsened, but there was nothing we could do and eventually we went in to bed.

In the morning the boat was lying on the sandbank as usual but deeper in the sand. We went out in the rain on to the windswept shore to inspect the damage. *The Puffin* had split her timbers in the night and by dawn the tide had been washing over and through her as she lay solid on the sandbank. Now that she could not float, it would be harder to bring her up for repairs and so she stayed there, wave-washed for a few weeks more.

Each day I came home from school, if it was high tide, I saw her wheelhouse appear in the troughs of the waves. At low tide she lay on her side bedded into the sandbank. I used to walk out and peer inside at the sand that had washed in through the split timbers. The sand was ribbed inside the boat as well as outside. It was as if the beach was devouring the crippled boat.

When the weather improved, Father gathered volunteers: Jack, Fred, Sammy, Willie Smith, Jackie, and Cecil, who had come on holiday from Belfast with his mother. He was very strong but a bit simple and had a soft spot for my mother.

On Saturday morning we all stood around the motorboat, lying aslant on the sandbank.

'Well, Tom, what's first?' said Willie, so Father allocated tasks: Jack and Cecil to haul on two thick ropes, others to lever the boat upright and yet others to push. I stood apart with Willie, who was calling directions: 'A bit left, Sammy; over right, Fred,' as slowly and painfully, they inched the bows in short bursts towards the shore. Whenever there was a surge of several yards, a shout of triumph went up. After a long hour, the boat had travelled fifty yards to the shoreline and everyone stopped for a break. Mother brought out a tray with strong tea and shortbread.

'That's a lovely tray, Missus,' said Cecil. She replied that it had been in her family for a hundred years. Grinning like a child, Cecil ran his fingers over its surface. Everyone else sat to smoke. Sammy and old Willie, both carpenters, sat apart on some rocks. I sat quietly behind them.

'He should have known better. That boat was lying out there for weeks,' said the younger man, lighting a Woodbine and spitting a piece of cigarette paper off his lip.

'Oh well, you know Tom. He always knows better. But, something happened, I think. The old man left in a desperate hurry,' said Willie, looking up at the darkening sky.

'The wife says he was a dirty oul …' said Sammy, then suddenly looking round and, seeing me there eating a Kit Kat, started examining the claw-hammer in his hand.

Resuming work, they managed to slew the boat round at right angles to the beach and pull it, stern first, high up the shingle. There, the two carpenters shored up *The Puffin* with planks, propping the boat on both sides. As each nail was hammered in, the sound echoed off the rock face of the sea wall.

The Puffin was now mounted upright in a wooden frame, her bow pointing out to sea, well above the tidemark. I thought she had never looked better, for even when afloat, she leaked and was always low in the water. After some talk of getting started in the morning we all packed up for the day.

That evening, I was happy to look out the window and not see the depressing sight of the sunken boat. We all fell asleep that night feeling satisfied.

Next morning I woke to hear sobbing somewhere. I climbed down from my bunk leaving Joss asleep in the tiny bedroom. In the kitchen I saw my mother standing at the sink. She wasn't doing anything, just standing there, her hands in the plastic basin in the sink. I told her I had heard crying.

'Not at all,' she said without turning round. I wanted to take a look at the boat before breakfast; they would be starting work on her soon. I stepped out the back door, the wet timber was lying ready for repairs. Then I went round the corner of the bungalow where a strong breeze hit me. I couldn't see the boat! And then I did. Back broken, she was lying smashed open, rising slightly as the waves washed though the wreckage. I stood and stared at it for a while, then went back to the house.

'Have you seen the boat? Where's Father?'

'He knows – he was out all night. He's gone back to bed.'

MY PARENTS had been wakened in the night by insistent tapping at their window. Outside was Willie, wild, white hair blown by the wind. Behind him was a huge expanse of angry moonlit sea. Father had stumbled out heading for *The Puffin*. Willie had been there waiting, holding a rope attached to the bows. The sea had been swilling around the supporting wooden baulks. There was no immediate danger to the boat, the rope Willie was holding was just a safety measure to keep the bows squarely facing the waves. He had indicated another rope for my father. There they had stood, eyes slitted against the wind and spray, on either side of the boat, taut ropes holding her tethered.

Suddenly a big wave swept up the beach and Willie shouted a warning. They found themselves waist-deep in water, struggling to keep their balance. As it swept back out, rocks rolling after it, the freak wave knocked away one of the baulks and *The Puffin* landed on the rocks broadside to the waves. Willie was already in the water, with his back to the boat, trying to get her bows facing the sea again, but my father got him by the shoulders and pulled him out of there. He had helped the seventy-year-old to sit down on the grass above the shingle and stood beside him. As they watched, a huge rock sucked up by the undertow was swung to a wave crest that broke over the boat and the boulder smashed through its bottom, leaving a splintered hole. Holed and broadside on to the waves, *The Puffin* stood no chance and in minutes the vessel had started breaking up.

By eleven that morning, the tide was out and my father got up. Red and white shards of *The Puffin* were strewn along the shore. One or two of the beachcombers had laid some pieces in front of the bungalow; we watched one of them, old man Irons. He was carrying a long piece of the planking in his arms and he laid it gently on the shingle in front of our house. With a brief glance at the porch window, he turned away and we watched him disappear round the sea wall.

When the wreckage was all collected in the back yard, like some funeral pyre, Mother started to use bits on the fire – and as I sat on the carpet playing with Meccano, we noticed that it burned with a good crackle.

MOTHER WAS in the kitchen drying the mixing bowl; suddenly it slipped and she screamed as it broke on the wooden floor. My father came out of the front room, saw the broken pieces and his wife sobbing that the last mixing bowl was broken.

'To hell with poverty!' Father shouted. My mother smiled through tears.

'Come on, boy,' he said to me, 'we'll go into Carrick. We'll take Tatty.'

The sky was overcast as we left the front gate and headed into the breeze off the beach. After passing Alan's beach house we negotiated the puddles of the dark lane between the poor brick houses of Boneybefore. With Tatty behind us, Father and I climbed the cinder path to Downshire and joined the main road to Carrick. We strode along, his hobnailed boots ringing on the road.

'Nobody attacks a hungry wolf,' he said out loud.

Passersby looked at us, noting his beard, beret and dog. They noticed too, his ancient hacking jacket, which Mother had recently dyed a wine colour. I asked him what he meant but there was no reply.

When we reached the town, passing under the shadow of the castle, we wandered down the quay. Tatty walked along the stone-clad edge, sometimes sniffing at a bollard.

'I heard about the boat, Tom,' a voice called up from below the harbour edge. We walked over to peer down. A big man in a donkey jacket stood in the middle of a fishing boat. It was Tony Cowan.

'Cowan, you Fenian bastard!'

'Well, how's the bearded beast?' he grinned.

Tony asked how we were going to fish now that *The Puffin* was gone and my father said that we still had *The Canary*, Pa's hundred-year-old boat. But, ignoring this, he asked Father about his writing to which he received a non-committal reply.

'Ah, catch yourself on, Tom. If you want to earn yourself a few bob, I'm out after herring tomorrow. Bring Ross with you.'

I was delighted. Tony said he would call by the beach on his way down the lough.

Next morning there was a strong breeze blowing. Father and I worriedly watched the tide become choppy and the sky grow overcast. Tony was late and arrived at one o'clock. *The Morning Star* chugged steadily towards the bungalow, then lingered fifty yards out with her engine ticking over.

We dragged the pram dinghy down the beach, then hopped into the tiny craft and Father rowed us out. The waves were tossing the dinghy and we were fighting a losing battle against the sea. Seeing this, the bigger boat moved round to shelter us from the waves and slowly we drew closer to the fishing boat and climbed aboard.

As soon as Father threw the dinghy anchor back, Tony turned the bow out to sea. Although it was rough, Tony stood relaxed at the helm. He was, as usual, wearing dark clothes and reminded me of the gunman in the song 'The Man from Laramie'. I had been singing it one day and when I sang the line 'gentle and kind was he', my father started laughing, asking if the man from Laramie was so kind, why had he so many notches on his gun. I had no answer to that.

I slowly became aware that the sea was getting up; we were well outside our usual inshore fishing range and heading into even deeper water. Father asked if it wasn't a bit rough for fishing and Tony, shielding a cigarette inside one hand, shrugged as he guided us with the other into the rising waves. He took a last drag and threw the remaining Woodbine butt into the sea.

My father's friend had a reputation: 'Are you not fishin' today, Tony? Isn't it rough enough for you?' was a shout we often heard down the quay. Tony had an intuition of where the fish were to be found and was demonic in his pursuit of them, even beyond the needs of his family, with nine children to feed.

'Are you writing anything these days, Tom?' he shouted over the wind.

Father, seeming not to hear, lay back in the stern lighting his pipe. I tried not to worry as the boat climbed a wave and we slid down a trough on the other side, I grabbed on to a ledge. I was getting nervous, but presently we came into the shelter of the Copeland Islands where the wind abated.

'I don't think we'll bother with the herring today; we'll shoot the trawl instead,' said Tony leaving the engine idling.

They let out the trawl net, a net bag that was towed along the bottom by the boat. As we ran before the tide, Father had started paying out the ropes while I stood watching. Without warning, a flying loop caught me round the ankle and I fell. Tony swore and stopped the boat just as I got the loop off. My father glared at me, but Tony was calm as we began trawling.

An hour passed as we worked a patch of seabed. Then came the call to 'winch in'. The two men managed the derrick and began to hoist the trawl, then swung the net of fish aboard where the squirming bag hung above the deck. Tony untied the end and a cascade of fish and seaweed poured down; some crabs clattered on the boards but in the middle was something large and active. Threshing about was the biggest conger eel I had ever seen: it was as thick as a man's arm and about five feet long. With the sweeps of its tail, fish were scattered everywhere. We all three reeled back in shock as a queer barking came from its ugly mouth.

'Jesus!' said my father and Tony asked him to pass a big spanner. I could not take my eyes off the huge conger; it felt as if I could not wake from a nightmare. Then Tony was shouting again for a spanner and Father passed him a large pipe wrench. Tony stood, slightly stooped, waiting his moment, then brought the steel mass down on its skull, caving it in.

'He's still moving,' I said.

'He'll twitch for a while yet,' said Tony and we stood watching its death throes.

Soon there was a rhythm going: shooting, then lifting the trawl. Carefully avoiding the now still conger, I sorted the fish into boxes as the other two worked the trawl. Eventually

Tony pointed up to the darkening sky and said we should head back.

We approached the open sea from behind the island and were met by chaotically high waves. I held on to the mast and watched Tony at the helm as the boat started rising up a steep incline. Then the stern was on the wave crest. Without warning, the boat dropped and split a hollow in two vast fans of grey water.

We were just clearing the island's edge when the engine failed and the boat started drifting back towards some cliffs. I saw Father looking up at the black rocks towering over us; he didn't look happy. I made a quiet vow, that if I lived, I would never, ever come out again with Tony.

The light was beginning to fail and when I felt sure that at any moment we would start breaking up on the rocks, a miracle occurred. The engine burst into life and we roared away out to sea into the worst weather I had ever experienced on a boat. Tony sat on the stern seat, both arms locked to the helm, as near immovable as he could be. I watched, fascinated at how he avoided the usual lift and crash by edging the boat over the wave in a slight roll. But the sea worsened and we had to return to the islands for shelter.

There, we sat tiredly in the open cabin, rocking in the darkness and waiting for the wind to drop. We were hungry and pooled resources; my father had a thermos of tomato soup and Tony had digestive biscuits. We drank the sweet soup, munched the biscuits, then lay back, resting. After a while the pair lit up: two glowing red ends moved in the dark as we sat well in out of the wind.

My father said, 'Jesus, that was rough, Tony. Didn't the *Victoria* go down near here?'

The fisherman didn't reply; I was remembering that Saturday morning in late January some years earlier. When I had woken, the wind was gusting against the house and there was a dull roar from rain pounding the roof. Then I parted the curtain beside the bunk to take a look and saw water pouring in rivulets down the window pane.

In the kitchen I found my mother, head down, listening to the radio. She told me that the Stranraer-Larne ferry was in trouble and there would be another bulletin at ten. I began eating my burnt toast and marmalade. When I had nearly finished, she turned up the volume.

This is the BBC News. There are reports of a ferry, the Princess Victoria, *with 172 passengers, in difficulties off the Scottish coast this morning. Two hours after sailing the Captain requested assistance from a tug and forty-five minutes later the ferry sent a distress message asking for immediate assistance. The destroyer* HMS Contest *at Rothesay, has been ordered to proceed with all haste to provide assistance to the stricken vessel.*

She and I listened all morning to the bulletins, each one grimmer than the one before. By late afternoon, it was obvious that many passengers had perished. The weather had cleared a bit, but the news was not good. One hundred and thirty people had drowned.

We learned that the *Princess Victoria* had left Stranraer on the south-west coast of Scotland but, not far from harbour, the stern gates to the car deck were forced open in heavy seas. Water flooded into the ship and, as the cargo shifted, the ferry (one of the first roll-on-roll-off designs) fell on to her side and within four hours had sunk. Rescue was virtually impossible, the ship was listing so much that no one could launch the lifeboats, some of which had already smashed against the ship's side. One lifeboat, with eight women and a child, was flooded by huge waves, subsided and was lost. RAF planes, hampered by sleet and rain, dropped rubber dinghies but to little avail.

There had been hardly any survivors. One man was found clinging to a raft on which were four others who had died from exposure. Among the lost was Mrs Hannah, our old cleaning woman from Trooperslane. She had been visiting her sister in Scotland and had delayed her original departure date by a few days.

I MUST HAVE dozed off for when I opened my eyes I saw a gap in the clouds through which the moon was shining down. We were moving again. As I stood, I saw the sea was calmer and the sky brightening. Eventually, through the cloud we saw the outlines of the castle a few miles off and presently we reached Carrick.

'Do you want to take her in?' Tony called to me. I looked to Father, who nodded. I aimed at the harbour mouth and managed to steer unsteadily through the choppy water in the gap. As we swept in, the slow, steady chug sounded against the stone walls of the deserted enclave. I looked at the boxes of fish and all the crabs in the bottom of the boat – more than Father and I would catch in two months.

Out of the wind now, we tied up at the wall and stood in the boat. I could hear my heart beating in the quietness. Tony lit a Woodbine and my father lit his pipe while I glanced, still suspicious, at the conger lying on the deck. Tony handed us the one lobster from the trawl.

'Take that home for your tea,' he said, 'Get some rest and we can go out again tonight. That was a nasty bit of water today.'

Father was stunned.

'Go out again – in *that*?'

'It'll calm down later. You wouldn't want to worry.'

'*You* can go if you like. You're not getting me out in that.'

'We have to go. There's not enough fish.'

'Well I'm not going.'

'Yes you fucking are!' said Tony and grabbed my father by the jacket. He shook his fist in his face.

'Let go, Tony,' Father said through his teeth, but instead of letting go Tony grabbed a handful of jersey with the other hand. My father's war training took over. Tony found himself lying on the deck. He looked surprised, then rage lifted him: this time he had a knife and he went at my father, who looked coldly at the spectacle of his friend in a blind rage. Tony hesitated and, sensing that my father was in a dangerous mood, stuck the knife into the wooden engine cover where it stayed quivering.

'I could do with a cigarette,' he said, 'Would you like one?'

'I have the pipe,' said Father, climbing the ladder up on to the quay. He took off his boots, one hand on a bollard.

The sun was rising, the sky was red. Tony sat down against a bollard and took off his shoes. Father eased himself down beside him and they sat there leaning against the same bollard. I sat down facing them.

'Could you not get your father to come out tonight?' Tony asked me.

'I'm off walking tomorrow,' Father said.

'Walking where?' said Tony in disbelief.

'I haven't decided. Up the country somewhere,' he said, puffing on his pipe.

'You're insane! Where will you sleep? You've no money.'

'I can sleep rough – in haystacks, under hedges. The weather's getting better. Today was a fluke.'

I looked at their faces bathed in the red morning light, the castle at their back as they gazed sleepily into the rising sun.

MY FIFTEENTH YEAR was the time of long drape jackets, brothel-creeper shoes and bootlace ties. The film *Rock Around the Clock* had provoked a riot at Carrick's Ideal Cinema – an unheard of event. Tennessee Ernie Ford's 'Sixteen Tons' – 'I was born one mornin' when the sun didn't shine' – seemed to suit the gloom of an Antrim winter but 'Que Sera, Sera' by the vivacious Doris Day was the essence of sunshine and happiness.

I spent Saturday mornings in Minorca, then the poorer quarter of the town where the Catholic chapel was. Near the bottom of a steep street I would turn right into a gap between the terrace houses, then come out on to a smoky grass-covered patch that looked down on the deserted brick factory far below. The big boys, usually Kenny, his brother and the weird Clegg, would be there on the rise smoking and talking about pigeons. Far beneath them in the valley lay the factory with its tall chimney, hollow-eyed buildings and slate roofs. That was where the card school was held. It was also where, one morning, Clegg had jokingly jumped on my back to ride me.

'Get out! You shouldn't be here, you're too young!' Kenny had shouted at me. Blushing and near tears, I ran back up the hill.

The next time I met Clegg was at a pigeon show: outside in the dark yard he appeared with his erect penis in a milk bottle. He could not get it out again. In the end he had, to our horror, taken a hammer and broken the bottle to release his member.

It was at Minorca that I learnt how to spit. This wasn't just ordinary spitting. The others had it off to an art: the spit was refined in the mouth by forcing it between the teeth until it was consistent, then, baring the top front teeth, you forced the spit between the two front teeth. It came out in a long fluid jet, a straight line to the ground. At first I couldn't get it, but after instruction from Kenny and daily practice I could do it perfectly.

One day at home, passing the porch I shot out the long fluid jet. There was a loud rapping at the porch windows and I saw Mother's angry face through the foliage of the geraniums. She opened the window, her face a mask of fury, and beckoned me over.

'Never, never let me see you do that again!' she hissed.

I ALWAYS WENT to Patsy's loft for the big Saturday races at the end of summer. Local pigeons were released from France to race home to Carrick. The biggest of the season was the so-called French Cup from Nantes. Patsy was in racing partnership with Flutter and although they were Protestant and Catholic respectively they worked well together, racing under the name Patterson and O'Reilly. They had already won the cup twice with a blue chequer cock, called King Billy, and they would get to keep it if they won this year too. Their greatest rivals were Flutter's brothers, Sean and Brendan O'Reilly, whose champion, Maebh, had come second to King Billy in a number of races. Flutter was the black sheep of his family for he had earned his name from gambling and was barely on speaking terms with his brothers.

On one particular race day, we were still standing at six o'clock in the evening sun waiting for the birds to return. Patsy's mother brought us out sandwiches.

It was about seven when King Billy, having flown several hundred miles, swooped down to land on the house's slanting slate roof. The bird stood there, then turned, facing down towards the loft, but saw Duffy the cat on the loft roof, who hesitated then stretched up, looking at its prey. Patsy reached down for a stone, threw, missed and hit the loft. Inside, the birds fluttered. The pair could win only if they got the bird's rubber racing ring off and into the pigeon clock. Patsy called, 'Come on Billy, Come on Boy,' but the bird hesitated and then the phone in the shop rang. Flutter ran to answer it.

'It was m'brother looking for news. I told him nothing.'

'Oh Christ – we must be in the lead. The fucking cat won't let him down,' said Patsy, throwing another stone. This time he hit Duffy, who yowled and disappeared. But the bird was now settled on the roof. Flutter was beside himself.

'Bring out thon wee French hen where he can see her!' he shouted and Patsy went into the loft. After a brief scuffle he put the hen in a basket near to the barred loft front. Then the racer made as if he would fly down but stopped, fluffed up his feathers and watched. The phone rang. This time Patsy answered.

'Their Maebh's back but she's still on the roof. Won't come down; they're doing their nut, he says.'

Flutter went pale and became very still.

'We can't let them win,' he said and went into the shop.

'Where are you going?'

Flutter came out with a shotgun broken open over his arm.

'Here, that's my gun,' protested Patsy but Flutter had already thumbed in two brass-topped cartridges. He snapped it shut, aimed at the racer and fired. We watched, paralysed, as King Billy fell like a stone to the yard.

'Get that ring,' said Flutter, shotgun pointing to the ground. Patsy did not move.

'Why did you do that?' he said hoarsely, looking furious and making to attack his partner.

'Pick up that bird – now!' Flutter shouted, pointing the gun at Patsy's stomach. White-faced, Patsy stepped forward, bent down and took the ring off the still-warm bird, then put it in the racing clock. The phone rang and Flutter answered it.

'We've won!' he said, 'Maebh won't come down.'

'You killed King Billy! I'll not forgive you for this,' Patsy said.

BY THIS TIME, pigeons were no longer my main interest, having been superseded by bicycles. I no longer had my original bike, which had been found by the river. It had served me well for I would often cycle up to visit Ma and Sadie, a distance of five miles. One day I was climbing the

Trooperslane hill when I felt a strange sinking feeling. When I looked down, I realized that, without a sound, the rippled frame had broken. On the train home from Trooperslane I was a hero as I explained to all the curious passengers what had happened. I didn't care about the bike. I was a cyclist now and knew that somehow I would get another frame.

One afternoon I saw a racing cyclist riding very slowly, at almost stalling speed, along the stone edge of Carrick harbour. He seemed to be unafraid of the sheer drop. I wanted to be like that man, but I still had no bike.

Sam Bailey, a new summer neighbour at the beach, brought me his own racing frame which was, he said, only gathering dust in his Belfast attic. He had been a racer in his youth and, although the Claud Butler frame was old-fashioned, it was good quality. I had built it up and gone round to show it to Paul, whose example I had followed in building my first bike. I was particularly proud of the gears, which had taken some time to assemble and fit.

'I'm taking mine off to put on a fixed wheel,' Paul said.

'What's that?'

'It means you can't stop pedalling,' Paul said, adding that you could balance at the traffic lights without moving. I suddenly thought of the cyclist on the harbour wall. Some of the evening riders down from Belfast I had seen in Carrick seemed able to stand still just when they felt like it. I had thought they must be acrobats or something. Now there seemed to be a secret – the fixed wheel.

So I, too, got a fixed wheel and, after much practise, was able to balance for a whole minute without toppling over. But I was soon to learn the one big truth of 'riding fixed', as it was called.

I had to collect a pigeon at Trailcock, which was uphill from the village. As I came back downhill, it was in a cardboard box, its claws scrabbled inside. Speeding down the hill, I gripped the handlebars but the box got jammed between my knee and the frame. The upcoming pedal threw me over the front of the bike and I landed at speed on my knees. The pain was excruciating and I roared my agony up at the sky. A woman came rushing out of her garden gate.

'Dear God! I thought there was a murder!' she said, her hand on her chest, 'Are you all right, son?' She sounded disappointed.

I nodded, and after peering into the box to see if the pigeon was all right, I painfully mounted, this time careful to keep the box away from my knees.

Each Sunday I would set off for a ride up the Antrim coast road, sometimes as far as Cushendall, where I met the Belfast cycling clubs, most of who brewed up tea in the woods outside Ballygalley. I was made welcome to join them and eat my sandwiches crouched among the trees beside their fires.

On weekday summer evenings the Belfast racing cyclists flew through the village towards Whitehead in pairs on a training spin after work. As night was falling, they could just be seen coming back, hurrying for Belfast before total darkness. Since they all had minimal lights – mere glows in the dark – they were wary of the police, who often lay in wait for them at this time. There was one very tall skinny policeman called Cecil Nairn, who was well known around the town. The unfortunate man had recently suffered a mental breakdown, with the result that not only did he look skeletal but his complexion was extremely pale.

One night he decided to catch some cyclists without lights and stood waiting in the shadows at the Scotch Quarter.

When he heard two approaching, he stepped out, flashing his torch. The cyclists were confronted by the spectre of a seven-foot, thin, white-faced figure looming out of the darkness.

'Christ, Frankenstein!' shouted one and they sprinted for their lives off into the dark, heading for Belfast as fast as their legs could push the pedals.

The Belfast cyclists also travelled down to meet the Carrick girls. On summer evenings, outside the Cygnet Café, pairs of cyclists cruised smoothly up and down chatting quietly. Occasionally a girl would be recognized and a rider would detach from his mate and stop for a conversation. Late in the evening there were sometimes long parting kisses, the man astride his bike, the young woman leaning in.

However, cycling was to become displaced by motorbikes. At weekends, I liked to help Mr Clarke, who lived along the beach. He was a dark-skinned, wiry man with horn-rimmed glasses, who had turned a narrow back bedroom into a real workshop. A trained fitter, he now had an office job in Belfast but metalwork was his passion. On Sundays, his brother would arrive with his glittering New Imperial V-Twin motorbike on which the pair worked together, bringing it to vintage perfection. The workshop walls were lined with neat rows of spanners and there was an electric drill high up in the work-shop, whose sharp tool cut into steel, sending oily squiggles of swarf writhing out on to his bench.

His daughter, Dorris, taught at Eden Sunday School where I had been a reluctant member. I was a few years younger than her and when I tried to borrow her comics, she would tease me, making me chase her round the Clarke bungalow. The worst of it was that her mother seemed to enjoy this flirtatious game too and giggled at my anger and frustration.

In the workshop hung a poster of the insides of an engine. The title was The Otto Cycle. It had four pictures: one where the mixture of petrol and air is being drawn into the engine, the next where the mix is compressed, the third picture showed the explosion with the spark plug and the last the burnt gases expelled as exhaust. I would stare at it as if it contained the secret of the universe.

'Disgusting!' said Mrs Clarke who had just looked in and saw me staring at it. Later I asked her husband why it was disgusting.

'You're too young,' he said.

'I'm fourteen, so I am,' I said, seeing from his face that he really wanted to tell me.

Once when I found myself alone with Mr Clarke's brother in the workshop, I seized the opportunity.

'What's so funny about that diagram,' I asked casually. Using a file in his hand he pointed to the pictures in quick succession: 'Suck, squeeze, bang, blow!' he said, grinning with evident satisfaction. I felt I was missing something, but tried to look knowing.

ONE AFTERNOON on the way back from school, I met Creighton. 'Do you know how to make fire?' he asked me.

I was perplexed. 'Come in here – till you see this.'

He led me behind a large bush by an unused gatepost in the lane. We squatted down and he took out his willy, spat on it and started to work on it with little groaning noises until it became big.

'What are you doing? I said, mesmerized.

'Making fire,' he said. 'Wait till you see.'

Someone walked by, just inches away. We fell silent in our green cave. The footsteps passed.

I thought his willy looked very big and red but I was getting bored waiting. Creighton was panting louder and looking up at the sky.

'Nothing's happening,' I said, getting up from behind the bush, making to leave.

'Oh, a big blonde with big tits,' he groaned.

'Does that help?' I said, puzzled, but Eddie was red-faced and panting when finally a clear whitish substance appeared at the end of his penis. I was surprised – I hadn't know that stuff was in there at all. I watched as he pulled a leaf off the bush and wiped himself. I was beginning to grasp the secret of the Otto cycle.

IRENE O'NEIL looked so pretty the day I glimpsed her on the school bus, dark curls showed under her beret. She got off at the place where the mustard-coloured Studebaker was parked. I loved that car – my mother said it was vulgar. It belonged to the butcher and was just like the ones in the films at the Ideal Cinema in Carrick.

Our first date was a hand-holding walk up Lovers' Lane.

'I love you, so I do,' she said.

I said nothing.

'With all my heart,' she said.

I thought it sounded as if she was reading it from a comic. She led me into a field that had a nice bank, where we lay down. I concentrated on getting my fingers inside her bra and she didn't stop me. After some heavy snogging, she rolled to one side.

'Look!' she said, craning her neck to look behind me. I twisted around and nearly died. We were surrounded by a group of bullocks staring down at us. I was terrified.

'Don't be scared,' I said, taking her hand and leading her through a gap in the hedge back to the safety of the lane.

'Don't be scared!' she mocked me. 'You were shaking like a leaf.'

That summer evening I got home late. Father was waiting.

'And where the hell have you been till this hour?'

I was paralysed.

'Tell him, tell him the truth,' said Mother as I looked at her in horror. He was already rising from his chair.

'I was … I was … with … a girl.'

There, I had said it. I braced myself for the blow, but instead his eyes grew wide with astonishment. He half-lost his balance and fell back into his chair with a thump.

'A girl? A girl?'

'Would you like a glass of milk and a biscuit?' my mother asked.

'Thanks, Mum,' I said gratefully going out to the kitchen.

A few days later I had just got off the bus at the Picnic Café when I met Eddie.

'Are you still going out with Irene?'

I said nothing. 'I met Spud Murphy down the quay last night. "Smell those fingers," he said, "they were up Irene."'

I went cold. That evening I would not speak to her but she finally got me to reveal what was on my mind.

'Wait till I get that Spud!' she said, her face and voice full of fury. But I would not be consoled and that night we broke up.

FATHER HAD now begun working on the lightship that was moored in the lough and was only home some of the time. On one of these occasions I was out trying to catch trout in the river. Legs apart, I was peering down in the water, trying to edge a fish into a trap. Back to the sea, I was facing upstream towards the bridge. Behind me the river spread out in a silver fan across the vast beach exposed at low tide. I heard the cry of gulls behind as I peered again. The fish was nowhere. Bert would be disgusted with me.

A posh voice spoke: 'Excuse me, do you know where Tam Skelton lives?'

I looked up: two well-dressed men were standing in the middle of the three-plank footbridge that sagged under their weight. The speaker wore a leather jacket. He looked amusedly down at me wading in the dirty river. His companion was dressed in tweeds and wore highly polished, brown shoes.

'We're looking for the writer, Tam —'

'Oh, that's m'father. I'll bring you down,' I said, squelching up the shingle riverbank.

'No, no, that's quite all right. We'll find our own way,' said the tweedy one, staring at my toes sticking out of cut-off canvas shoes. 'Just show us the house, would you?'

'Ah no. I'll bring you down m'self,' I said. Leather Jacket grinned.

My parents seemed excited and I quietly watched the ensuing dance of the adults. I soon gathered that Leather Jacket was Louis MacNeice and he seemed to be the more important one.

The tweedy man spoke.

'Do you do much fishing this time of year, Tom?'

'Well, I have longlines out and a salmon net.'

'Really?' said MacNeice politely. 'How long is a longline?'

'As long as a piece of string,' laughed the tweedy one.

'They can be a thousand hooks – maybe a mile long,' my father said, visibly warming to his subject. Mother and I, and probably MacNeice too, had heard this speech countless times before. He started enthusing about fishing and then on to his favourite subject: 'I've a fully paid-up salmon licence – unlike a good few around here,' he said, not mentioning the fact that he could hardly earn the cost of it back from fishing.

MacNeice and his friend listened politely, even contributing from time to time. Then they fell silent. Years later I came upon the poet's line in *Autumn Sequel*, 'a thousand excitements flapping on a thousand hooks', and wondered if it arose from conversations with my father over the years.

They stayed for tea. Sitting round the oval kitchen table, I watched as MacNeice moodily kept turning his herring over and over with his fork. The only noise for some time was knives and forks on plates. Suddenly there was a bang on the wooden roof above the table. The poet and his friend looked upwards in surprise.

'It's just one of Ross's pigeons. Would you like some more tea?' Mother said.

'Pigeons? Homing pigeons?' the poet exclaimed, his face coming to life for the first time.

'They're out the back. D'you want to see?' I asked.

'I'm sure Louis isn't interested in them,' said my father.

'I'd love to see them. Show the way,' said MacNeice, getting to his feet.

'I'll stay,' said Tweedy as if indulging an enthusiastic child. 'Louis likes pigeons – God knows why.'

I opened the latch on the back door next to the table and

the poet followed. The pigeon loft faced us. I turned and looked up at the roof of the bungalow where the bird had just landed: it was my dark blue chequer cock.

'Come on boy. Come on!' I called, rattling a tin of pigeon beans. The bird flew on to the loft and stood on the landing board, the sun catching the green and purple sheen on his neck. Then he dropped through the bob wires and flapped down inside the loft where a chorus of cooing broke out.

'I had pigeons once,' the poet said, peering through the bars.

The back door opened; Tweedy and my father joined us.

'Couldn't miss out on the pigeons, Louis,' said Tweedy smiling.

'Tam, didn't you have a borzoi bitch? What was it she was called? Some Russian name,' the poet asked.

'Natasha – we call her Tatty; she's over there,' said Father leading us away from the pigeon loft to the side of the bungalow. There, dejected, stood Tatty, hair all matted, chained to the doghouse. Her food bowl was full of slices of white bread floating in some liquid; other slices lay on the ground. Only the day before I had counted seven rats creep across and drag slices of bread away below the bungalow. Tatty had not stirred.

'Here Tatty! Here Tats!' called Father and the skinny dog picked her way across the corrugated iron enclosure, floored with dogshit, mud and bread. She had a swelled stomach: we couldn't afford the vet, so her condition had got worse. I saw Tweedy's eyes widen. The poet turned away and walked down the side of the bungalow and out towards the sea.

'How's the writing, Tam?' he said softly. At first Father didn't reply and his face took on a wintry look.

'Things are a bit slow. The BBC said they wanted me to do a few features. I sent one in. At the last minute they said it was unsuitable, but then that's the BBC for you – and there was that other feature I was promised and never a word since. Why they treat me like this I'll never know – my essay on selling herring was chosen for an English textbook – I've got letters from everywhere about my stories … my play too. The rejection said 'either you're a genius or the world isn't ready for you.'

We had all walked out to the path in front of the bungalows and stood surveying the shore. The tide was half in; a flock of racing pigeons landed on the sand.

'There's the main gillet there,' said Father, pointing to a river far across the sand. 'I set the net across it to catch the salmon on their way out on the tide.'

'Tom!' Mother called from the house. 'Jackie can't start his bike. He needs a push; it won't take a minute he says.'

When Father came back, he was still panting from pushing the motorbike.

'What's that out there, Tam?' MacNeice asked, pointing towards a row of black dots on the glittering sea.

'That's my nets – all paid for. I've a full salmon licence, unlike a good few around here.'

'It's just as well there isn't a poet's licence. We'd all be in gaol for breaking the rules,' he replied and Tweedy laughed. 'I'm up at the BBC tomorrow. I'll see if they can make an opening for you, Tam. We must get together some time soon,' were MacNeice's parting words. Father perked up and Mother looked adoringly at the poet. As their backs moved away down the path, Tweedy said something and they laughed. Father was cheerful for the rest of the day and that evening he announced, 'Louis won't let me down.'

The next week Father was away working on the light-ship. Tatty was getting worse and one afternoon after school, I watched her unable to stop the rats stealing the pieces of white bread that were now her meals.

Some weeks later I had returned from school and was feeding the pigeons. A train was passing behind the loft when my mother beckoned me over. The noise of the train was fading away as she spoke between her teeth. Obviously, I thought, it was something secret and I couldn't hear her.

'What?' I said loudly.

Mother gave me a warning look and spoke out of the corner of her mouth.

'Daddy's dead!'

My first thought was happiness: he was dead! But she looked calm – normal even. I tried to look suitably shaken.

'Oh, for goodness sake, what's wrong with you?' she snapped. My God, I thought, his death is nothing to her!

'Daddy's dead?!' I repeated.

'No, silly – *Tatty's* dead.'

Since Father was away on the lightship, she and I had to bury the big wolfhound. We dug a huge hole in the garden for her large body and shovelled earth in on top of Natasha's stiff white and black coat.

'At least she's free now,' my mother said.

ALTHOUGH I could not aspire to owning a motorbike, my fascination with engines grew and the Clarke brothers got me an old engine to work on.

As I began to dismantle it, the strange parts of the engine emerged from its dark innards into the daylight. It was like when I had first seen codfish on the longline swirling up from the deep, more strange to me than beings of another galaxy. True, I couldn't put the engine back together, but the experience was joyful and full of surprise. Before long, I had become engine mad and could always be found working on the bench in the backyard among Father's tools.

'You'll marry an engine one day,' my mother would say, watching me covered in oil.

Now I lived for engines and, unbeknownst to me, they were to radically change the course of my life. At the time I had still not given up Meccano and one evening I was building a robot on the floor. My father didn't like robots; he said they gave him the creeps. As I worked on, bolting together the red and green pieces of metal, I could hear him – that incessant scratch, scratch, pause, sigh of him writing. Occasionally, I would cast a glance in his direction.

On one particular winter's evening he had stopped writing and, laying aside his pen, turned up the radio and began listening intently to Mendelssohn's 'Fingal's Cave' overture. Apart from the occasional clink from my Meccano and the sound of Mother's knitting needles, the room was filled with the swelling music.

'That man didn't write that music!' Father exclaimed when it had finished.

'What do you mean, dear?' said my mother, looking up from her knitting.

'It was written *through* him.'

'You mean from the Beyond?' said my mother, humouring Father's mysticism.

'From the Beyond – from *beyond* the Beyond!' he said triumphantly. Watchful from my place working on the floor, I saw Mother wink at me and I must have smirked. I was always careful to hide such signs for I knew the electrifying effect this had on him, when his anger quickly rose to violence. But he must have seen it for he stood up.

'Well, what are you going to do for a living, boy? Do you want to be a butcher, a baker, an *engineer*?' he said, looking distastefully down at my Meccano robot. I examined every detail of the boot near my face and the steel studs in its sole. It wasn't really a choice, but from past conversations I knew that being an engineer meant leaving home and I had never been away from the beach.

'What's wrong with the shipyard?' I said hesitantly.

'There's no future here. No son of mine is going into that shipyard!' he replied, and for once my mother nodded in agreement.

I knew that all this talk about going away was connected to my bad marks in school and I would certainly not be going to Queen's University, Belfast. If it was anything like school, I didn't want to go there anyway. I didn't even know what a university was or what people did there, for neither of my parents nor any of our neighbours or friends had been to one.

Later that week, as I lay on the floor among Meccano pieces, Mother thrust a writing pad and pen into my hands.

'Your father said to write off for the RAF brochure. There's the address!'

Perplexed, because suddenly it was supposed to be my responsibility, I started writing the meaningless letter on the floor among the bits of Meccano.

'Why can't I go to the shipyard?' I asked.

Mother's face was set.

'Well, why can't I serve an apprenticeship in Bristol Siddeley, like you said?'

'Your father's looking into that,' she said, tailing off.

Before long, the RAF brochure arrived in the post. On the cover was a dramatic photo of an armourer servicing a guided missile, the kind of thing to excite a fifteen-year-old. I was excited but suspicious too.

Despite my mother bringing the Bristol Siddeley option up at mealtimes, Father showed no interest and somehow the whole issue of the civilian option faded.

During this period something unexpected happened. I got

home from school to find that someone had slashed Father's canoe. He was devastated.

'Who would do that? I haven't an enemy in the world!' he said, horrified at the damage to his beloved canoe; he looked at me.

'It wasn't him!' Mother said fiercely, startling both my father and myself.

As the Bristol option faded, family opinion hardened in favour of the Air Force. Now, when the subject of joining the RAF came up, I was told it had been my idea. A shadow slowly began to fall on my mind and each day now seemed blighted. Whenever I got nervous about joining the armed services, I would take out the glossy RAF brochure and look at it again. Life in the Air Force looked good but part of me knew it wouldn't be at all like the picture. Finally a letter came offering me an interview but, although it was only a preliminary one, I still felt I was being sent away to something horrible.

ON THE MORNING of my departure for the interview in England, I had only gone a few minutes up the lane when my mother caught up to me and, breathless, handed me some money. She looked strained and I could see she didn't want me to go. It started raining.

At the bus stop were two women who knew me.

'He's very young to be going away, so he is.' I heard one say to the other as they climbed on the bus and the other turned to stare at me. When they got off at Carrick, I was alone upstairs in an empty bus watching the wind-torn sea through raindrops on the window.

At the Belfast recruiting office, I was greeted by a smiling

Squadron Leader. I didn't like him. Then the small group of us for interview were taken off to the boat train for Larne. I was surprised when it flew through Carrick station and passed Eden Halt, for my mind was already focused on what lay ahead at Halton camp in Buckinghamshire.

As the boat train from Stranraer to London bucked and swayed though the night, we played cards. There were four of us with the sergeant: Dessie, Harry, Terry and myself. Dessie, tall and skinny, could twist his mouth in funny ways. He burst into song: 'You ain't nothin' but a hound dog …' The others didn't pay any heed and kept playing.

'Are those the only words you know? Flush!' said Terry, a rotund, good-natured boy, showing his cards.

'Busted,' said Harry, a weasel-faced ginger, 'How about you, Sarge?'

The sergeant and I silently handed in our cards.

'I wonder what it'll be?' said Terry. 'Will we have to march all the time, Sarge?'

'Call me Paddy,' said the sergeant.

'My uncle says the drill square is the worst – they give you hell,' added Harry. The sergeant was quiet: a velvet glove. Mother had warned me that sergeants were the mailed fist. She had even tried to prepare me by getting me to march up and down our small sitting room. I had laughed at her and she had cried, but she had seemed so distraught that I had sensed it was a warning.

'Are you a drill sergeant?' I said before I could stop myself. The RAF man started but quickly got control.

'Everybody does a bit of drilling,' he said.

'Are you going to drill us?' Dessie suddenly asked, making a weird expression by twisting his mouth.

We laughed but the sergeant looked uneasy.

'You are, aren't you?' I chipped in and the sergeant blushed; we all looked at him. From then on, all the way to our destination outside London, no one called him Paddy any more.

AT RAF HALTON we were shown into a long billet where the gleaming brown linoleum reflected twenty steel-framed beds. Some of the beds were already taken. I started unpacking my hold-all.

'What's that?' said Terry staring at my red silk pyjamas, 'Are you rich?'

My heart sank. Mother had insisted I take those pyjamas with me. They had been among the second-hand clothes from Joyce Grenfell that had arrived at the house years before.

'My mother made me take them – I hate them,' I said, but by then the others had come to look. I knew what would happen: I would become different again.

The sergeant strolled in, saw the red pyjamas and shook his head in disbelief.

'What's the likes of you doing here?' he said.

That night, I was sitting on a scrubbed wooden toilet seat; the cement floor had been scoured and I marvelled at the cleanness of everything. As I sat there in partial darkness, two airmen came in, their steel-tipped heels ringing on the concrete floor.

'What's in there?' one remarked.

'Some fuckin' little rook,' his friend replied. The tone of the remark cut into me and in that moment, I knew what was in store: I, too, was to be a cleaner of lavatories.

I stood outside the toilets feeling I just wanted to go home and forget everything. Already that day I had seen marching airmen being shouted at on the vast, windswept drill square.

'Are you one of the Irish?' a soft voice called, it sounded just like Sean in school. I turned around and down the stairs came a pasty-faced, overweight young man.

'From Antrim,' I said.

'Homesick already?' He seemed to read my mind, 'Come on upstairs. I'll show you around. I'm from Dublin – Paddy Swift.' Upstairs, he took me to a window and together we looked down the dark valley at the patterns of little square lights in the camp buildings. He turned to face me.

'You don't like it here, do you?'

I shook my head.

'You'll get used to it. *Nil carborundum* – don't let the bastards grind you down!' he pronounced.

NEXT DAY, I noticed that I got more interviews than the others, but finally a genial rattlesnake of an officer said: 'Skelton, you've been a bit of a puzzle for us but we're going to give you the benefit of the doubt.'

I nodded. The talons of the Air Force eagle pierced my flesh.

Still shaken by the experience, I got back home a few days later to find my father in the front room talking to a schoolmaster friend, Bill Hazlett, who taught what were then called 'mentally deficient' children and referred to himself as a mentally deficient teacher.

'All right was it?' my father said as if I had just come back from fishing. Beyond feeling anything at that point, I retreated. There was no welcome here. My father was giving the impression that he had hardly expected me back.

'How was it, Ross? Did you have a good trip?' the school-master asked, turning around to smile at me. It was better than my father's silence. I went into the kitchen, where my mother embraced me.

THE WIND had blown all night and, as usual, I had slept through it. At breakfast, I sat down to eat my burnt toast and noticed that BBC Northern Ireland was playing instead of Radio Athlone. I asked Mother why and she replied that there had been a hurricane in the night. Jimmy Reid's shipyard had been lifted off the harbour and just dropped on the main road in Carrick. Then she handed me an envelope with a horrible little black crown on it. I knew what it was: an acceptance letter from the RAF. I left it down and continued with breakfast; some crumbs and a blob of marmalade fell on the envelope.

'Aren't you going to open it? Go on!'

I picked it up. Sticky-fingered, I opened it.

Dear Mr Skelton,

We are pleased to inform you that subject to passing your Junior Examinations, you will be admitted to the RAF as an aero engineer. Please confirm in writing by 23 March.

Yours sincerely,

T.N. Roberts

Squadron Leader

At first I didn't feel anything, then, as the weeks passed, a feeling of dread at being taken away from this beach slowly took me over. The shore was my world. I had almost never been away from it. The rhythm of the tides were mine, individual rocks were my familiars, I knew the bay in all its moods, from mirror calm to raging gales. I began to ask Mother to get me books on inshore marine life from the library and she obliged by bringing home anything she could find. I pored over the books and walked the shore, drinking it all in, knowing that it was over: the smell of the seaweed, the screaming of the gulls, the high tides and the low tides – especially the low tides.

My last visit to the Tangles at half past five in the morning was solitary. It was a spring tide and the sea was over a mile out as I crunched down the shingle. At that time the Council was laying a sewage pipe over the sand and out to sea. Three men were working at low tide, using a steam piledriver to hammer the supports down through the sand and deep into the clay base. The regular thumping of the steam hammer echoed across the beach as I walked to the ebb. The tide was a mile out and the piledriver's noise receded as I crossed the vastness of wet sand.

When I reached the Tangles, I discovered that the sea had gone out unexpectedly far, exposing rocks I had never seen before. They were covered in a kind of yellowish skin from being in deeper water. Excited by all this virgin territory revealed by the spring ebb, I began exploring the new field of tangles.

I soon spotted a large, flat boulder, at the side of which a burrow of sand had recently been scooped out: the sign of a lobster. I took my gaff and gently offered it into the hole. There was an empty silence, no audible, sharp snap as the gaff was gripped by a lobster.

Disappointed, I kept searching and instead caught a few crabs, using Mother's intrepid method of scouring around under the weeds on rocks.

After an hour I noticed a slight scum had begun to form on the water – a sign the tide was on the turn. As I walked away, I had one last lingering look around. I stumbled and nearly fell but steadied myself by grabbing with one hand on to a nearby rock. On closer inspection I saw it was two rocks leaning together, forming a tent-like space between them. I peered down into the water: side by side rested a large hard crab and a soft-shelled one. Next to its hard-shelled partner, the soft crab glowed with an eerie ultraviolet light. With a slight pang of conscience, I drew out the hard-shelled one, leaving its vulnerable mate alone.

As I headed towards home, walking the mile or so towards land, the piledriver was silent. I began to hear the sounds of the wakening world: the occasional car engine starting or the hoot of a diesel train. By the time I reached shore the world was awake.

Keenly aware it was my last summer, I had been doing a lot of fishing, using a longline pegged on the sand. But the crabs were stealing the bait. I told my father, who said that there was a way of avoiding the problem. It was a method he had learned from Pa. It worked only when the sunset and full ebb were occuring at the same time. Then he went into soliloquy mode: the flatfish he had caught – the size of dinner plates; he had filled a bucket with them.

I asked if we could do it. He was doubtful but Mother reminded him it was nearly the end of the summer. At such times he would go quiet, the only sound his chewing. Then he would take two gulps of tea to drain his mug before speaking.

'I'll have to check the tides,' he said, getting up to fetch the tide table book. After consulting it he told me to dig the bait and take the boat out on the tide the next day.

The morning was warm with a haze over the high tide. We could hear the small summer waves drop on the beach as Mother and I had our toast and marmalade in the sun on the front steps. Occasionally, there was the sound of a leaping salmon splashing back into the glass-like surface of the bay.

After breakfast she helped me heave the wooden rowing boat down the sloping shingle and ease the bow into the water. As morning wore on and the tide slowly fell, I kept pushing the boat out to keep it afloat. When the first sand-bank was dry, I took the garden fork and began digging the hard sand for bait. After each forkful I would bend down and pull out a fat lugworm.

Over lunch Mother refused to discuss the RAF, so I went back out to more digging. Soon I took a rest and looked around. Water was flowing out in streams under the shallow sea: the gillets. When the tin was full of worms, I took it back to the house and left it under the shade of the bungalow. Then, sitting on the shingle, I idly watched sea birds on the wet sand and in the pools of the ebb tide. Far off in the distance our rowing boat bobbed on a shining sea.

With bloody fingers from hooking worms, I gathered up the baited longline. Then I carried the coils a mile out from shore and pegged them down on the sand with short wooden stakes.

By then the tide was on the turn and the sun low in the sky. In the distance I heard the sound of Father's motorbike. I walked back to shore and arrived just as he cut the engine and lifted his aviation goggles.

'Everything's ready,' I said. To my surprise he did not speak but looked thoughtful.

'No, you go on your own,' he said.

When I had recovered from my surprise he reminded me to bide my time, that if a fish got hooked, to wait a bit until the others came to see what had happened and then to stab the biggest.

I ran the half-mile to the tide's edge just in time to wade out to the rowing boat, now veering with the slight current. It was deeper than I'd thought. I seized the bow, levered myself up into the tilted boat and took up the oars. As the boat drifted before the incoming tide, the water was only a foot deep, I felt like a tiny cork bobbing on a vast, shallow sea.

The sky was darkening and the red sun bleeding into the sea when I spotted the marker buoys of my line. I picked up the stabber from the bottom of the boat and, quietly shipping the oars, allowed the boat to drift over the line. As I peered over the side, the boat tilted alarmingly but down in the shallow water I saw that a big flatfish had already been hooked. It looked very big and was struggling to get free of the hook. To my surprise, and exactly as Father had said, other flatfish had gathered around to see the commotion. His words, 'Bide your time', came to me and I waited until I saw the biggest spectator, then thrust the stabber through it.

I pushed it off the tip of the stabber and into the bucket. A few times more and the bucket was half-full. The sky was quite dark now and a light breeze sprang up. It was hard to see, so I pulled in the line and took off the already hooked flatfish before heading for the light of the bungalow.

I steered the boat towards the clear patch of shingle in front of the house, and soon the keel ground against the stones. A dark figure was waiting on the shore – my mother.

'THAT LOFT will have to be taken away,' my father announced the following week at dinnertime, going on to say that old Irons might give a few bob for it. I sat trying not to exist and looked at my mother, who was staring at her plate. Only a year earlier I had redesigned and amended the front almost every week until I got what I considered to be a perfect loft front. All the best driftwood had gone into it. Now it had to go. I was shaken by the suddenness of it all.

My mother was unusually breezy about it. Obviously she and my father had been talking.

'Aren't you going to sell that pigeon basket?' she asked me.

'Can't you keep it for me?' I replied, for I was proud of it, having chosen it carefully after months studying the black and white pictures in the *Pigeon Racing Gazette*. Varnished wicker, it had a brass plate riveted on the top with our address on it.

'What use would we have for it?' she asked.

Patsy said he would give me a price and the next Saturday I arrived at the shop with the basket. He came out wiping his mouth, glanced at the basket on the counter and offered me a pound. I was shocked; it had cost me six. I pointed out the engraved brass plate.

'That's not my address on it — no good to me. Thirty bob.'

Defeated, I took the money.

ONE EVENING while we were eating dinner, there was a soft knock at the back door. Mother rose and opened it. Old Irons was there.

'Tom, I'm down about the loft.' My father got up, wiping his mouth on his sleeve and I followed him out to the yard. The three of us stood looking at the loft. My shoe was in a puddle. Irons wanted to know why we were selling and Father told him. Old Irons looked at me as I felt the wetness in my shoe. Suddenly I didn't want to be there. I took a step away. Father was offered two pounds and accepted immediately; it felt as if he couldn't wait to be rid of me.

'He's very young to be going away,' Irons said, looking over at me. My father shifted on his feet.

'There's no work here. Men must work and women must weep,' he announced.

The next day Irons and one of his sons arrived. I could not bear to look and stayed down the shore and tried to skim stones. None of them skipped more than two hops. While their donkey cart waited outside, the Irons took the loft apart in minutes and I saw the donkey and cart jogging up over the railway line.

When I got back, there was a gaping space, with just the biscuit tin full of pigeon beans on the ground. From then on, each time I went out the back door there was no greeting from the pigeons: just the presence of a big empty hole where the loft had been. No longer was there the comforting sound of the birds walking on the wooden roof of the house or the bump when they landed home from a race. I had given my pigeons to Bert, who in later years was to become a consistent race winner in the Carrick area.

IN SEPTEMBER 1957, on the morning which I had come to regard as the day of execution, I was wakened by the foghorn at Blackhead. When I looked out the window, little could be seen beyond the hedge. After my last breakfast, Father and I stepped out into the chilly morning.

'Goodbye, darling – and write!' Mother held back her tears.

Outside we could not see very much, but tiny waves could be heard tripping on the shore and the sun shone dimly. The beach was quiet and no one was about because most of the men had gone to work. Here and there I could make out individual boulders on the shore.

Father was striding ahead as if he could hardly wait to get it over with. Sassy, the old labrador, plodded along through the mist beside me. We were last across the three-plank bridge to Eden Halt.

'Come on, Sassy!' Father called as, threading ourselves through the wooden railway gate, we mounted the cinder-strewn Halt and stood, backs to the sea, looking into the fog. Neither of us spoke. The silence began to grow tense.

'I'll not wait. Good luck, boy!' Father said, turning to go. I got down on my hunkers and looked into Sassy's unseeing eyes.

'Bye, Sassy,' I said, thinking that she would not live long. She wagged her tail slightly.

'Come on, girl!' Father called and I had to chase her away. Tears started to come to my eyes. As he crossed the bridge, Father raised his walking stick in the fog – a farewell salute.

When they had gone, hearing the train in the distance, I peered up the parallel shining lines into the thick fog at Kilroot. Seagulls cried to each other as I got up into a carriage and stood looking out the open window. I heard running and saw Mother coming out of the mist. She came panting up the Halt.

'You forgot this,' she said, cradling in her hands all the coins I had left behind on my dressing table.

'I don't need …' I started to say, then saw her grief-stricken face.

'Take it! Take it!' she shouted over the noise of the train's diesel engine as the lit carriages drew alongside. As the train droned out, I let down the window and looked out at my mother disappearing into the fog.

I WAS BEYOND FEELING. When Harry, Dessie, Terry and I boarded the Larne-Stranraer boat train at York Street Station, after waiting most of the day in the RAF recruiting office, I still felt nothing. We stopped briefly in Carrick station, and I sensed that Mother would be standing there somewhere waiting for her train home from the library. I did not attempt to look for her but kept my attention on the card game. Harry was winning but I was hardly aware of the game.

Out of the station, the train speeded up and by the time we were passing Eden Halt, I just glanced out at the bungalow roofs below. On our roof, motionless, stood nine-year-old Joss. I jumped up but he was gone and I returned to our game of cards.

'Was that your house?' said Terry. I nodded.

Over the years that followed I was always annoyed that my brother, Joss, would never speak about my departure. One day, I caught him off guard and asked him what it had been like after I had gone. He replied in a word: awful!

It was the force of feeling concentrated in the word 'awful' that made me curious. Later, after dinner, we got drunk at his house and, as his wife slept in the kitchen armchair, he began to talk.

That day, he confessed, he had come home from Eden school and looked in the cold oven: he could eat all the left-over breakfast crusts now that I was gone.

Mother was home first and did not speak. She had busied herself making dinner and when Father came in, he had been greeted by a wall of silence. They sat down for dinner as Mother hovered over the stove and handed the dinners round the table.

'Mum, you've made Ross's dinner,' Joss had said. All three of them looked at the full plate before the empty chair.

'His train stopped in Carrick station when I was waiting to come home. I looked for him, but I couldn't see him,' she said, scraping the dinner plate into the dog's dish. As she stood up, Joss saw tears streaming down her face and started crying himself.

'The Father looked stunned watching the two of us in tears. I suppose he knew that he would never be forgiven,' said Joss.

WE SLEPT FITFULLY on the train from Scotland as it bucked and swayed through the night. Drawing into Crewe station, I was mesmerised by the multitude of silver railway lines curving into the dark. When the train finally stopped, I rose to buy tea and biscuits through the window from an urn outside the carriage. My fellow recruits, as well as our RAF sergeant escort, stirred from their awkward slumber.

'What's the time?' asked Dessie, the gangling youth.

'Half four,' replied the sergeant, lighting a cigarette.

'Shut that window,' said Terry, 'some of us are trying to sleep.'

Tea drunk and windows closed, I had scarcely subsided into another fitful sleep when we arrived under the canopy of Euston Station. A brief trip on the underground took us to Baker Street, where we joined a quiet crowd of strained-looking sixteen-year-olds carrying holdalls, waiting on the platform for the Wendover train.

Our journey ended at a small sleepy station where we were spewed onto the platform. Our steps thundered over the footbridge to the exit. We were met by an exceptionally polite corporal, who directed us to the waiting coaches in the car park. When they were finally filled up, they took us the few cushioned miles to barracks. I had been astonished to be called 'mister' by the corporal and, although we did not know it, in a matter of days we would be referred to as 'orrible little men' and shunted into the back of trucks for bone-shaking rides on wooden slatted seats. I had no idea of Halton or its history except that it claimed Sir Frank Whittle, the inventor of the jet engine, as one of its own. As we slowed for the Guardhouse, I could see a sprawling array of brick buildings in the shadow of dark hills. These, I was later to learn, were called The Chilterns.

OUR IRISH GROUP was deposited at Block One where we were shown our quarters, just below ground level. The long room had high windows and a deeply polished, brown linoleum floor that reflected the outlines of twenty steel beds, ten on each side of the room. To the left of each bed stood a squat wooden locker and to the right a narrow wardrobe. I picked the second bed on the left, which was to become home for the next three months.

When the others went off to the toilets, I found myself alone in the company of a thin, dark boy and asked him where the other inhabitants of the room were. In reply, he pointed out the window where about twenty youths in faded khaki overalls, bunched at the waist and ankles, were stumbling by in a macabre semblance of marching.

'Fli–ight – Halt!' roared a short sergeant, puffing out his chest. In their confusion the pathetic-looking youths bumped into each other.

'Le–eft turn! – One poles two!' called the sergeant.

'One poles two – one poles, two poles!' they shouted in ragged unison, shuffling awkwardly into line. I stood stunned by this bizarre sight of frightened, chanting recruits. It was alarming, the confusion on their faces was palpable and I felt like running. But where could I run to? Certainly not home, since I had been effectively sentenced here by my father for fourteen years. In any case, I would have been brought back by the military police. There was no escape.

I expressed my fears aloud.

'Go on – be a devil!' the dark youth nudged me and, seeing no way out, I offered myself up for what in my mind had now assumed the dimensions of a human sacrifice.

The recruits had been dismissed and were scrambling into the building and the sergeant told me to pick overalls from a pile. After changing I joined in the next episode of unsteady confusion.

'What's this one-poles-two stuff?' I asked a tall boy, who introduced himself as Reg.

'What's up, Paddy?' he replied, catching my Ulster accent.

'Shut up Irish or I'll have you on a bloody charge!' shouted the sergeant. I was already a marked man.

'It's one *pause* two, you idiot,' replied Reg from the corner of his mouth as we attempted to march off in step and promptly bumped into one another.

When we got back from this humiliation, I found the thin, dark boy still sitting on the bed except that now a case was beside him.

'Why weren't you with us?' I asked.

'I'm going home – I don't like it here,' he replied with a smirk. We had a special word back home for people like him: 'sleekit'. I was speechless, I didn't like the camp one bit either and this individual had been the one who had encouraged me to join in. 'Be a devil,' he had said and now he was deserting me. He was leaving and I could not – or at least the idea was unthinkable for me – to go home and face the father who had sent me away.

On the first morning I was wakened, not by the waves thundering on the shore at home but by the brassy sound of Reveille trumpet call outside the billet.

'Hands off your cocks and on with your socks!' shouted Iggy, the snag or apprentice corporal, who lived in a separate single room at the end of our billet. With a creaking of metal springs, we all leapt from our beds, bare feet on the brown lino. Ablutions were conducted in a long, stone-floored cold room where, in our underwear, we washed at a row of white basins before running back to our bedspaces to struggle into our denim overalls. Boots tied, we grabbed our so-called eating irons, which consisted of steel knife, fork and spoon on which was stamped our service number – I was 683515 – a number I shall never forget. In my mind it felt like the branding of steers in cowboy movies – smoke rising from burning cowhide. The large white pint mug was the exception and I acquired an affection for things without numbers.

We poured down the stairs and ran outside to stand in line, then, holding irons and mug behind our backs, Iggy marched us to breakfast.

'Atten…tion! Left turn – by the left quii-ick march! Right wheel!'

IN THE CAVERNOUS, dark canteen we queued up for breakfast and peered at trays of solidified scrambled egg made from powder and niggardly bacon scraps. From metal urns, strong tea, released by a tap, gushed into our pint mugs. It was rumoured that the tea had bromide in it – something to quell sexual appetites. After a few months, I would discover that there were some Venezuelan apprentices among us who had their own special imported coffee which they were happy to share with me. I would then luxuriate in my breakfast of cornflakes and milk washed down by the excellent coffee.

Immediately on return from the mess, the drill sergeant would be waiting for us. With hardly any time to leave our eating irons down, we were marched to the barber and made to queue up outside. Each time one of us emerged there was a gasp at the severity of the haircut. It was the beginning of the Elvis era and hair was being worn longer and thick at the back, reaching its end either as a 'DA' (duck's arse) or a Boston (shaved across the collar in a straight line). Eventually I took my place watching others in the barber's chair. Pluglug (he had a hearing-aid) did not bother with scissors but took a large electric razor and with five swoops up the sides of the head, the victim's hair cascaded onto the floor, covering the barber's shoes.

When my turn came, I looked in the mirror. Was that me? I hadn't seen my reflection for what seemed like ages and a familiar feeling of existing came back into me. Pluglug raised his weapon and I felt it scour up the side of my head. I closed my eyes and when I opened them a stark creature greeted me from the mirror.

INITIATION BY searing haircut completed, it was time for PT and the instructor told us we were going for a cross-country run in the hills. It was only a few miles, but fairly tough even for myself, fit as I was from miles of beachcombing at home. I was astonished when, high in the hills, we were allowed to stop for a smoke. Nearly everyone had brought cigarettes in their denim pockets and, lighting up, we had ten minutes of normality. Even the PT instructor lit up, before extinguishing his unfinished cigarette with his fingers and slipping it in his pocket for later. Face tensed, he barked us back into formation and soon our boots started drumming on the road back to camp. For the next three weeks we were to have long periods of PT, interspersed by endless spells of marching.

At the foot of a dark, wooded mountain lay the parade ground, Maitland Square, around which stood our gaunt brick billets. As the camp lay in the shadow of this mountain, the sun never shone on our accommodation until mid-morning. A wind blew through the shadowed canyons between these red-brick edifices, chilling us as we headed for parade. In my memory, the square always had a cold wind blowing across it and the marching commands on the square: 'By the left – quick march!' or 'Squadronnn ... Atten...tion!' were often bent in the wind.

Our drill instructor, a Sergeant Davidson, was a small dapper man with red cheeks, who stuck out his chest, displaying his rows of medal ribbons. Marching did not agree with me and he soon singled me out for his sarcastic comments.

'You're the only one in step, laddie,' was the mildest of his sniping, which seemed to be directed mostly at me. Another instructor, Corporal Newton, was more perceptive.

'You're fed up Paddy – aren't you?' he would hiss in my ear.

'No, Corp,' I lied.

I later learned he had been busted down from sergeant and was himself very keen to leave the service.

'Paddy – I can't see anything wrong with your marching,' said Reg, the gentle giant, my first English friend. It was true that my marching was poor but so was that of a good few others – it seemed I was being picked on.

ALL OF US IRISH – Dessie, Harry, Terry and myself – were called Paddy and it was not long before we had acquired a reputation. It happened the night Harry had the idea that the four of us should go to The Astra, the camp cinema. When we returned at ten, we found to our astonishment that everyone was hard at work polishing, scrubbing and cleaning.

'Here come the reasty Irish,' someone shouted and there was a roar of agreement. We had not known it was 'bull night' (scrubbing and polishing the whole billet) and had innocently taken the evening off. It was some time before we lived that down but there was never again any sign of real prejudice that I can recall.

ON MY FIRST DAY, returning at the end of this punishing routine, it was raining. Several hundred of us assembled, wearing tent groundsheets – ugly, brown oilskin poncho-style garments. Through the slanting rain I could dimly see a solid block of apprentices approaching from the direction of the airfield. Wearing oilskin coats, they looked incredibly confident but the odd thing was, they did not swing their arms. I gaped as they halted near us.

'Who are they?' I asked incredulously.

'The 79th,' replied Reg, 'they're up from Airfields.'

Airfields was the most senior class of all, where apprentices learned hands-on experience with actual jet aircraft before graduating to the real RAF on the outside. These top dogs of the senior entry were to become our models and I was still marvelling at their arrogant stance when we were rudely called to formation: 'Get fell in, you fucking shower!' shouted one of the runts as the pipe band struck up.

'By the le-eft – quick march. 'Eft, 'eft – 'eft, 'oight, 'eft.' His voice pierced our tiredness and we trudged off in the pouring rain. Inside the phalanx I looked around at ground-sheets glistening in the dark and wondered how I had ever managed to land up in this shouting world. As we marched up the hill in the night, a drummer's single beat punctuated the darkness. Just as the band struck up with the customary drum roll, the whole of the senior entry – the 79th – scuffed their feet in unison and then again after the second. 'Brr-rr-um' went the snare drums; 'Scuff-scuff' went the 79th boots; 'Brr-rr-um' they went again; 'Scuff-scuff' … This, I was to learn, was their unofficial prerogative. The bagpipes struck up with 'The Black Bear', which put a spring in our tired step before we were back to silent marching with the single drumbeat. Without warning a lone shout rose in the night:

'Who are the boys who make most noise?' And a hundred voices took it up: 'Hoo, Raa, Hoo, Raa-Raa … 79th!'

This conveyed a strong expression of power to the rest of us. Only the senior entries were allowed these shouts, and only the senior entries did not swing their arms. We were the rooks, they were the Gods and to this day, when walking, I always avoid swinging my arms.

THAT FIRST WEEK had blitzed our minds, to what extent I did not realize until the first Sunday came around. I woke that morning and leapt out of bed but to my disbelief everyone else stayed in bed. Was I going mad? What could they be thinking?

'For fuck's sake, go back to bed, Paddy,' said Reg, 'it's Sunday.'

It was some time before it sank in: Sunday was actually a free day! It seemed unbelievable after a week of barking orders and endless verbal abuse, but finally I relaxed and sat on my bed until the others stirred. We spent Sunday luxuriating on our beds, reading the *News of the World*, eating doughnuts and drinking Tizer, a soft drink from the NAAFI (Navy, Army and Air Force Institutes).

WE WERE KEPT intensely busy from six in the morning when the Reveille trumpet sounded, until 'Last Post' and lights out at ten. This meant that most of us were too exhausted to think of home. We stumbled from one form of discipline to another until we hardly knew who we were any longer. Sometimes I would wake in the night amidst twenty other sleepers to hear someone sobbing. Others too, must have heard but it was never mentioned in the mornings, for I think all of us knew exactly how the person felt. At lunchtimes we would return briefly to the billet and open the swing doors, anxious to see if there was a small white square on our bed – a letter from home.

My first letter was dominated by Mother's account of a storm that had torn some boards off our wooden bungalow and blown down the paling fence. That same afternoon, she wrote, a herd of cows had come along the beach and started grazing in the gardens. Since my father was away at sea, working on the lightship, she had to cope with all this herself and had driven the animals off, even managing to re-erect the fence with some help from the postman. Tears came to my eyes but the call to parade outside put paid to any emotion.

After that first white-hot week we were sufficiently melted down to be poured into our new identities. On Monday morning, we were lined up to be fitted for uniforms. From being anonymous clones in boots and denims, we were now identical boys in blue. In time, promotions would begin among us and we would be revalued and judged by the small stripes (or lack of them) on our arms. Two hundred of us apprentices stood queuing in the rain to get into the clothing store. Inside was a long counter with sweating storemen sizing us up by eye before thrusting a rough uniform at us. Then back out again to queue outside another wooden hut, the baggy coarse serge sawing against our skin.

'Next!' called the corporal.

Inside the tailor began slashing my misshapen blue uniform with his flat tailor's chalk. While he worked he talked cheerily and I had the impression of a man with unusual zest for life. As I was leaving he told me he had been rescued by the Allies from a concentration camp.

Now that we had uniforms, we also had brass buttons, embossed with crown and eagle, to clean. Every day, the natural corrosion on the brass had to be wiped out, polished away. I always used to think of the brass ship's bell outside our bungalow at home, which was never polished and swung ringing in the wind. None of that here, all had to be neat and tidy, as if anything natural had to be stamped out and wildness exterminated. At night, because our blankets were in the pack, the bed had to be made anew, so in the morning the pack had to be made again before breakfast. We would learn to wet the creases of our trousers and lay them carefully beneath the under blanket then we would have perfectly pressed trousers in the morning.

It took several weeks to polish our rough new boots up to standard; evening after evening we sat on our beds alternately spitting and rubbing in black polish, until the boots resembled patent leather. I had never before had to do anything quite so mindless, for the life I had left in Ireland had been the opposite of this insane polishing. Our house had been very untidy; life on the beach had, apart from school uniform, been lived in old clothes and nearly everything I wore was in holes or heavily patched. And as for haircuts, at home I rarely had one at all, whereas now we were shorn regularly like sheep. Then there were the frequent inspections.

'Stand by your beds – Atten...tion!' roared Iggy, the apprentice corporal. In strolled the flight commander, Lieutenant Brownlow, holding his leather gloves in one hand. Behind him glowed the red face of Sergeant Davidson. Mine was the second bedspace on the left and I stood to attention beside my bed. At its head was the blanket pack – a perfectly folded oblong sandwich of bed covers. On the remaining space my equipment was spread out in the geometric pattern we had been taught. The officer gave it a cursory glance then turned over my mug with the end of his swagger stick.

'Sergeant, why is this man's mug filthy?'

'Corporal?' echoed the sergeant.

Iggy, the swag corporal, looked blank.

'There's shit in this mug!' said the sergeant holding it up to my face. I looked inside – it was white and clean.

'It looks clean to me,' I said. There was an awful silence.

'Don't answer back! I'll ask you again, laddie – why is there shit in this mug?'

I decided to say nothing. The birds were singing outside. The sergeant looked apoplectic and Iggy, the corporal, went white.

'Put this man on a charge, Sergeant – where are you from, apprentice?'

'Northern Ireland, sir. What am I charged with, sir?'

'Dumb insolence!' snapped Davidson and without warning smashed my mug against the iron bed end. The shards skittered across the polished linoleum, one curved piece rocking gently where it came to rest. Meanwhile, the officer had gone behind me and was feeling along the ledges in my wardrobe for dust. I was almost certain there was none and, looking to find fault, he came around me to look in my bedside locker. Inside were the official folded clothes. He reached in to the back and drew out a yellow book.

'A book. Books are supposed to be in storage.' He looked at the title. '*Zen Buddhism* by Christmas Humphreys,' he read aloud and exchanged glances with Sergeant Davidson. 'An Irish Zen Buddhist? – God help us!'

THE INDUCTION PERIOD ended with a full dress parade on the drill square that was, as usual, windswept. Three hundred of us stood in formation, shivering for an hour as we waited for the inspecting officer. Eventually a staff car arrived and the wing commander, immaculate in his tailored uniform, began slowly strolling with his retinue along our files, looking each apprentice up and down. Occasionally he would stop to criticize or ask where someone was from but he was still far from my group, or flight, as it was called.

During the long wait I watched, fascinated by the tenor drummers in the pipe band. Led by the drum major flourishing a magnificent mace, the band was marching up and down the square, the white sticks of the tenor drummers whirling complex patterns in the air. So engrossed was I in watching that I did not see the danger approaching. Suddenly they were upon me, Davidson's red face glowering behind the Wing Co.

'Where are you from, apprentice?' A refined accent – another world. I thought of the Rothschild mansion, now housing the officers' mess.

'Northern Ireland, sir,' I said and he looked at me with fake interest.

'Some of our greatest generals, Ulster,' he said airily.

'Who, sir?' I asked. Davidson's eyes widened.

'Oh, lots of them,' said the officer, quickly moving on to the next victim.

'– and straighten that tie, apprentice!' snapped Davidson as he passed. I moved to correct my tie.

'Not on parade!' he said between gritted teeth. The retinue moved on until it was a murmuring farther down the ranks. We were now coming into the third hour standing and I began to ease myself up onto the balls of my feet to relieve the strain. I began to drift off into what I fondly imagined (from reading my book on Zen) was a state of 'no mind'.

I was woken from this reverie by the dull heavy thud of a body falling on the tarmac – someone had fainted. I turned slightly to see two apprentices carry the unfortunate apprentice to the edge of the square. There, the two helpers stood over the man who, now sitting up, had revived.

'Fuck this for a lark,' muttered Reg beside me.

By the end of the third hour we were doing the final 'march past' in long straight lines perpendicular to the dais. There stood the inspecting officer saluting as we, on the march, twisted our heads in unison to face him in an 'eyes right'.

EACH MORNING, headed by the pipe band playing 'Cock o' the North' or some such, a winding snake of several hundred blue-uniformed figures marched downhill to the workshops. Our marching was accompanied by a lot of shouting from corporal and sergeant apprentices: 'Get your arms up – left, left – left right left.' From the sleep-laden safety of the ranks we softly told them to fuck off. On our left was the camp commandant's cream-painted house. Down in a hollow, surrounded by trees, it seemed to me to belong in another world – a place of peace where we would not be shouted at by the runts that were in charge of our march. On our right was a high fir-tree covered bank called Skates alley, used by apprentices late back from drinking to avoid passing the Guardroom.

It was cold, very cold, and clouds of white breath rose from our ranks when we reached Main Point. As we soon learned, this was where the station warrant officer or the duty officer lurked, waiting to find fault with any aspect of our being. These officers, usually junior and hungry for promotion, could airily call you aside, make you stand to attention, and demand to know why a coat button was undone or boots imperfect. This was all done with a kind of aristocratic air that officers at that time affected. One particular man, a flight lieutenant called Harrison–Broadley, specialized in picking on berets. Apprentices, especially the more senior ones, prided themselves on having an old faded beret which conferred status on the wearer. Harrison-Broadley would call such a person aside, tell them their beret was a disgrace and rip it up on the spot. Marching up from work in the evening the station warrant officer, a rather perverse skeletal creature called Joe, would demand to know why someone was not wearing a beret.

'Flight Lieutenant Harrison-Broadley tore it up, sir,' was the usual reply and Joe would nod sagely. The rumour abounded that this officer had been demoted and was anxious to be promoted back up to squadron leader. Many years later, I heard that after leaving the RAF he had become a prominent member of the British National Party.

ON ARRIVAL at workshops we were divided up into different trades: airframe, engine, armourer or electrician fitters. I was in the engine group where, back in khaki overalls, we were alphabetically assigned to instructors. I found myself next to Jock Riley and six others, under the instruction of Fred King, a civilian.

Standing by our stations at the workbench, next to a vice, we were all handed a rough block of mild steel, a bit like a rusty lump of iron railing and told to file it into a perfect block accurate to within one thousandth of an inch. From that day on, every morning from eight to twelve we filed and filed – our whole attention focused on the lump of mild steel gripped in the jaws of the vice. We were allowed to talk as we worked but we longed to be outside for our tea break. This was when a hundred or so apprentices, all in khaki overalls, milled around waiting for the sight of the NAAFI van. A cheer would go up, the side hatch opened and two girls would dispense tea and doughnuts that, after two solid hours of filing, we all consumed ravenously.

This process was to take weeks, whole mornings of filing and checking if we were a 'few thousandths' up or down on a surface of the five-inch block. Fred, our instructor, was on standby and helped willingly, although he had a wicked sense of humour. If someone was a fusspot for accuracy and asked for too much help from him, he could take up a coarse file and, to the dismay of the toady apprentice, remove too much. This effectively stopped anyone trying to insinuate themselves with him, and he remained resolutely aloof.

Whereas the march down in the morning was somnambulistic, by midday we were starving and the march uphill at lunchtime was very fast. We would come though the swing doors to our billet, stuff any letters left on our bed into our pockets, grab our eating irons and run for the mess hall.

A remarkable feature of billet life was that there were no chairs. If you wanted to sit, it had to be on your bed (or pit as it was called) or someone else's. After lunch we would read *Titbits* or the *Daily Mirror*, leaning back on our blanket packs, until it was time to march back down to Schools. There we were taught by officers who, recently graduated from university, were now doing their National Service. We covered mathematics, science and technical drawing as well as endless RAF history. Unlike the career officers, our teachers were enthusiastic, if a bit naïve. They also they had no military attitude, which I, for one, found a relief.

AS CHRISTMAS APPROACHED, discipline slackened and a very strange thing happened in the billet. As if in a dream, we instinctively formed ourselves into groups of three or four and, using lockers and wardrobes with blankets pinned between them, formed small 'houses' within which we lived like families. To me it seemed an act of anarchy and I was certain we would be ordered to take it all down. But it must have been some kind of tradition for no one ever interfered and a Christmas spirit prevailed inside our cosy improvised caves. I think we secretly longed for privacy for almost every act was public; even the toilets had foot-high gaps at the bottom and we were only free in our dreams. Christmas provided an opportunity for us to create families again and to enjoy privacy.

Finally we were given week-long passes for leave and we Irish set out for Euston to take the boat train to Heysham. My memory is of the smell of spilt stout, crying babies, drunks, vomit and climbing over people sleeping on the floor.

When we drew into Belfast docks it all seemed an anti-climax and more so when I arrived home in uniform, on a Saturday morning. Amidst humorous comments about my short hair from Mother and Joss, Father was more guarded in his welcome.

'You expect flags and bunting to welcome you, but there is nothing,' he said, alluding to his own return from the war, twelve years earlier. I sensed relief, though, in Mother's warm welcome when I told her I was home for a week. My brother, Joss, was curious.

'What's it like?'

'All right,' I replied shortly.

In retrospect I must have been still stunned by the tough discipline. I felt unreal and separate at home – it was as if my body had been away but my feelings had never left, yet they seemed paralysed. One thing I definitely appreciated at home was the presence of chairs!

Christmas itself was uneventful; Father had got one of his 'special' turkeys for the meal as usual. Neither my brother nor I could ever see anything special about 'our' bird and suspected our gullible father was probably being cheated by some cute turkey breeder. But at dinner we all sang the turkey's praises and Father and Mother both looked pleased. In my absence nothing had changed at home except that Father had bought a blue van, now parked out on the triangle of rough grass above the shore.

In the afternoon I walked up to see my friend Bert and found him in his pigeon loft. I climbed the steps and went in. He smiled but looked at me strangely – as if I wasn't me any more. Later, when I went through Eden village, a few doors opened.

'God, Ross – is that you? Are you back, then? How long are you staying?'

But after saying hello, no one seemed to know what to say next and I began to get the feeling that although I was physically back, I had been written off in people's minds. They seemed to just look through me, it was as though in going away I had stopped existing.

Next day, I took the bus from Eden to Smithfield market in Belfast. In the summer evenings before enlisting I had cycled there with my friend Paul to look in the bike shop windows. Outside Raymond's Cycles, which was closed at night, we would gaze at a royal blue track frame in the window. On Saturday afternoons I would hang around the shop and talk to Raymond, who held court over the counter. Unable to afford it, we often talked about his shop window centrepiece – the blue Claud Butler track frame.

Today, I walked through the market and up to the shop: the Claud Butler was still there! Raymond had promised it to me for £16.

'Hello Raymond,' I said, jauntily stepping inside the shop, 'is that Claud Butler track still sixteen pounds?'

'Where have you been?' he replied, staring at my short hair.

'Away in the RAF – is the frame still sixteen?'

'Sixteen,' said Raymond cautiously. It was clear he didn't want to sell – it had been the centrepiece of the window for over a year. I took my hand out of my pocket and handed him the still-warm folded bank notes.

'Can I have it then?'

Almost in shock he opened the shutter to the window and took out the frame.

At home, the Claud Butler had pride of place on my bedroom dressing table where I would just gaze at it. During that Christmas week I put on wheels and assembled it. It was a beautiful, smooth, responsive ride. I had not known cycling could be like that.

From time to time I noticed Father's van. It didn't look too good and I soon saw its new coat of paint was covering deep rust. I had a peep inside — the floor was half corroded away and it had a familiar smell, reminding me of hens. As Joss and I watched, my father and Robert, Bert's father, who was a mechanic, got the engine going. After belching black smoke, it subsided and spluttered to a halt.

'Where did he get that thing?' I asked Joss.

'Some farmer called McCosh up the country. I went with him. Would you believe, it was in a field being used as a hen-house. We had to chase all the hens out of it. "She's a great engine" your man said and the father believed all of it. Mother says it was fifteen pounds and now we're stuck with it.'

But Father was full of it and, undeterred, he and Robert worked all week until the old van went the length of the beach backfiring and belching black smoke. On the Saturday morning, when I left, they were having another go at getting the henhouse on wheels going and as Mother, Joss and I walked along the beach to the station, in the distance we could hear the old van backfiring.

BY THE SECOND YEAR at Halton, a few of us apprentices had realized that there was a world outside the monastic RAF. One friend was showing a gift for engineering way beyond anything the RAF would require. Another, Tich Harper, a diminutive folk guitarist, began vanishing into the night with his instrument and his tall skinny henchman called Millie. Together they visited and played the folk clubs of the area, climbing through the window at the end of the billet at all hours. Tich clearly was following his private muse, which would lead out of the RAF and to his distinguished career as the famous folk singer, Roy Harper. Meanwhile, I myself was following my own drumbeat, although it was still faint and far away.

One of the things that had annoyed and perplexed my literate parents was that I read very few books and as a young teenager was mostly absorbed in comics like *The Hotspur*, *The*

Rover and *Superman* which a boy in school got from America. Nor did I read newspapers like *The Manchester Guardian* or *The Observer*. At Halton I read the *Mirror, Titbits, Blighty* and *News of the World*. But I was slowly changing.

At Schools, one afternoon a week was now devoted to an endless series of films: *War in the Air,* or the gruesome footage of bulldozers clearing up dead bodies after the concentration camps were opened up by the Allies. When I could stand no more of this material, I asked the Education Officer if I could have permission to read instead. To his credit, he agreed and from then on I became a solitary figure reading in Halton's well-stocked, otherwise empty library. The officer rarely checked on me and when he did I was busy reading T.E. Lawrence or something on philosophy – a subject on which my father expounded at home. As a young man, Father had been a street preacher but in recent years he would, at the drop of a hat, hold forth on his reading in esoteric literature to the baker, the postman or anyone who showed the slightest interest.

One day I took out a tiny book, *The Problems of Philosophy* by Bertrand Russell, whose clarity of expression was the polar opposite of Father's gnomic utterances. Such was Russell's charm and skill as a writer that I was soon drawn into doubting tables still existed while concealed under tablecloths. I then graduated to reading *Introduction to Mathematical Philosophy*, a book Russell had written while in prison. I have no idea what drew me in such a strange direction, nor had I any idea what an effect reading these books was to have on my life. Flying officer Pethick, our mathematics teacher, was astonished when I asked him about the Russell-Frege definition of number. But, above all, what I found so appealing about this form of logical philosophy was its clarity and precision of argument; whenever Father wasn't doing well in argument, he would declare: 'Well you're as far as you're near!' or 'You're as big as you're small!'

BEFORE LONG, many of us were travelling farther than the local area of Wendover or Aylesbury at weekends and before long we discovered the delights of London.

My first experience I will not forget. One of us knew a man who could 'get girls'; we had wandered aimlessly round Leicester Square and into the Haymarket, then our contact motioned us through a doorway and up a rickety staircase. My demands to know where we were going were ignored as we climbed to the top floor. 'Is this it?' someone asked. On a door was a piece of jotter paper affixed by a drawing-pin, with 'The Haymarket Club' written in pen and ink. The door opened, and we were all introduced to someone called Jack. Inside was a spacious room, where six or seven young women were sitting on a bench. They rose as one and started towards us – a dark pretty one fixed her eyes on me. Then an argument broke out about money and to my relief we left.

Soon I began to make trips alone which included visits to art galleries and the so-called art films that were to be seen at The Everyman, Hampstead and Oxford Street's Academy cinema. There, on Saturday afternoons, I saw the work of Ingmar Bergman, recognizing in its moaning winds and stark landscapes an echo of my Protestant Ulster origins. The films of Buñuel appeared at this time and, although I found them perplexing, I enjoyed such images as the gas pump attendant becoming Pope or a flock of sheep being driven into church.

One in particular stands out in my memory: a film about the sculpture of Henry Moore, in which his works had been placed on the Yorkshire moors. The famous parental work called 'King and Queen' framed against the sky made a deep impression on me.

On Sundays I mostly went to art galleries, mainly for the paintings but I had also discovered that many au pair girls spent time there. I soon found a method of lingering by a picture and making a casual remark to a girl who, probably bored by her time off from looking after young children, would be glad to have a date in a strange city.

Looking back on this London period, it strikes me that I was always alone; but it never seemed that way to me at the time, for I was absorbed in a mission: I wanted to become educated. Back at camp I longed for London and by my third year I had perfected a method of escaping early, thereby avoiding Saturday morning parades. After breakfast, while the others were getting changed for the drill square, no one ever noticed a lone cyclist slip out the back way of the camp. I would not be caught absent on parade because the Sergeant would assume I was playing with the pipe band. But I told the band I would be with the squadron and, since they never cross-checked, I could be somewhere else – London – only half an hour away on the train.

One such Saturday morning I had cycled out of camp as far as Great Missenden railway station where I parked the bike and sat down on the wooden railway bench. As I basked in the morning sunshine, up the line I could hear the clink of shovels on rough stones from workmen on the tracks just beyond the platforms. I began reading my *Times Literary Supplement*. Three young people came down the platform – two men in tweed jackets and a girl who was asking one of the men about some mutual friend.

'Oh, he was at Cambridge but got sent down,' replied one. My ears pricked up at the name of the university. They chatted on, occasionally glancing at me, the apprentice mechanic, reading the *TLS*, probably taking me for a student. I raised my eyes from the page and gazed up the railway line; the workmen were resting on their shovels in the sun. It came to me: I could go to a university. In retrospect, before joining up, I remember reading the brochure I had been sent by the RAF, and in it was a picture I returned to again and again: an image of an officer holding a sheaf of notes, evidently explaining something to a student. This was virtually a picture of my future career as a university lecturer.

ON GRADUATION FROM Halton I was posted to RAF Stradishall in Suffolk and soon became accustomed to the screaming of jet engines and danger of working with armed fighter aircraft. But the desire to go to university was becoming stronger. I had never been inside one so I decided to visit nearby Cambridge to watch a Footlights performance. This raised my enthusiasm for universities even higher and I cycled the fourteen miles home in the dark with a firmer resolve.

Reading through the newspaper one day I came upon an advertisement for the Rapid Results College. I was keen to study for A level French and English and after I sent off the cheque, began receiving my 'lessons' by post. The English course began with *Piers Plowman* and my essays seemed to meet with approval or at least encouragement. They would arrive rolled up in the post and I would open them during working hours in the oily, smoky, crew room to the cat-calls of the others: 'Got your homework, Paddy?'

As I continued to study, I enjoyed the English course, particularly Chaucer's *Canterbury Tales*, but began to fall behind in French, which was a bit advanced for me. To catch up, I hit on the idea of locking myself in the lavatory to learn the long lists of vocabulary. But since there was only one toilet, this caused a lot of annoyance when other technicians wanted to use it. Unsurprisingly, I was also harassed by people from the combat airstrip wanting me to go out and work on the aircraft. Eventually I relented and dropped French but my mind was made up. I had sworn to be out of the RAF by the time I was twenty and although I meant it, I had no idea how to do it.

DURING THAT YEAR at Stradishall we were on Cold War surveillance detachment in both Libya and Cyprus. I had one firm friend at this time, Pieter van Raat, and we were bound together by our loathing of military life. When we returned to Britain he tried to persuade me to desert to Sardinia. I refused, so he promptly went AWOL, climbed London Bridge and threatened to throw himself off. This got him a discharge from the RAF on psychiatric grounds. Deprived of my friend and ally, I decided I would try to get out in a similar fashion. In the back of my depressed mind a plan began to germinate.

Around this time there were a lot of night-time exercises which involved refuelling planes taking off and landing from dawn to dusk. My sleep patterns disturbed, I felt groggy during the day. To make matters worse, I had also started to sleep in my clothes. Back on day shift I could not sleep at all and after another week of not washing I reported sick one morning and told the medical officer I could not go on. He sat up, alert, and began quizzing me on my health. I told him I hated the RAF. Why, then, he asked, had I joined up? I replied that I had been 'joined' up by my father when I was sixteen. He did not respond to this but asked me to come back after I finished work that evening.

After a day of avoiding as much work as possible I reported to the Medical Centre. In the waiting room I was surprised to find two of our ground crew, Yorky and Mac. They started chatting to me about Operation Matador, the large NATO exercise coming up soon. While we were talking I noticed the medical officer's door was open and had a sudden intuition that he was eavesdropping, so I worked my discontent into the conversation, ending with the declaration that I simply could not face Operation Matador.

After my colleagues had left, the medical officer told me he would give me a sleeping cure for depression. He told me it would take some days to take effect, and then a medical orderly escorted me to a bed where I was given some pills.

I later learned that, at that time, long spells of sleep were prescribed for depression. I slept for two days solid. On the evening of the second day, Yorky and Mac came to visit me but I was unable to stay awake long enough to talk and was allowed to sleep on till the following morning. When I tried to get out of bed, I could hardly stand and barely managed to walk along the narrow corridors of the centre, arms outstretched, using the walls for support. Eventually I found a quiet spot in the sun at the emergency entrance and sat down.

As I sat in a reverie, contemplating the grass through a haze of drowsiness, a blue Land Rover screeched to a halt. Sleepily I watched an officer lead an ashen-faced airman towards where I was sitting. I vaguely noted the man's finger was hanging off.

'Come and help! Oh, get out of the bloody way!' he shouted as, too slowly, I gathered myself to move away from the door. When they had gone, I settled back sitting in the sun. The officer reappeared and had clearly been talking to the medical officer for he looked at me with mild alarm.

'I didn't realize …' he tailed off.

'Hate the Air Force,' I said and solemnly tapped my forehead with one finger. He looked at me with pity; clearly you had to be mad to hate the RAF.

Next day I was more alert and the medical officer enquired how I felt now about the Air Force. I told him I still hated it.

'That's what I wanted to hear,' he said. 'You're going to Ely Hospital tomorrow.'

Yorky and Mac from the squadron drove me to Ely, promising to come back at teatime to collect me. I deposited myself in a waiting room and after a long time I was called in to the psychiatrist. As soon as I sat before his desk, he fired off a few brusque questions. I explained that I wanted to get out of the Air Force and again I was asked why I had joined up. I gave the same explanation but he said he could find no reason for me to leave the RAF. I was stunned but then he hesitated.

'I'll just go and consult with my boss,' he said and left the room. A frosted glass window was open and I stood up to look out. The sun was shining on a burst of nasturtiums in a small enclosed garden. Mother's favourite flowers.

As I stood waiting, my mind went back to a day in the Libyan desert – a few of us were sitting in the shade when a black scorpion appeared. Pieter, my Dutch friend, poked at it with a stick keeping it at a safe distance as its bite was fatal.

'Wait till you see this,' he said, reaching for a can of Avpin – a high octane starter motor fuel. He carefully poured a ring in the sand around the scorpion, then reached into his pocket, drew out a lighter and lit the fuel. A ring of fire appeared on the sand and the tiny, lobster-like creature tried to escape in one direction, then another and again until, increasingly desperate, it seemed to realize there was no escape.

What happened next was riveting: it stopped still, tail arched over its back and stung itself to death. It had committed suicide. My train of thought was interrupted by footsteps – this was it, I thought, the whole course of my life was in the balance.

The doctor swept in.

'It's OK – you're getting out. It's all fixed.'

I had done it!

It would be two hours before I was picked up, so I wandered round the hospital grounds until early evening in a state of disbelief that it had been so easy.

Basking in the red sunset, I waited on the hospital steps for the RAF Land Rover. Above me on the balcony a woman spoke.

'Wave to the nice man,' a nurse was saying to a young child. Me? A nice man … it felt strange – as if I had become an individual again. It was like those days, so many years earlier, growing up on the beach.

Back at camp I particularly looked forward to returning my tools to stores; this was, for me, a symbolic act. When I got there with my tool-box I was confronted by a half-door with a shelf. I knocked, the top opened.

'What do you want?' a corporal with an Irish accent asked.

'I'm getting out – returning tools.'

'Leaving?' He looked at me sceptically, 'Where's your authorization?'

When I produced it he looked disappointed.

'Could you sign here please?' I said.

He paused, then looked carefully at the release form as if wanting to find it suspect, then, realizing he had no choice, signed it. But he didn't give up there.

'What will you do with yourself in civvy street?'

'I'm going to study – get to university.'

He seemed nonplussed but rallied.

'You'll be back,' he said. 'They all come back.'

He seemed so certain it gave me pause for thought. Years later I realized what he meant: the one thing you gain in the armed services, often missing in civilian life, is comradeship which is different from friendship. It must have to do with shared hardship for even though camp morale in Suffolk was generally low, in the Libyan desert the shared bleakness of our experience had seemed to bind us closer.

YORKY DROPPED ME at Haverhill station around teatime and wished me all the best. Soon I was sitting on the local train, feeling the heavy vibration of its diesel engine through my whole body; it was just like the train at home. One young woman with a child looked my way with evident interest. She could not have known what that look meant to me; it was a welcome – a welcome to the normal free world where your worth is infinitely more than the stripes on your arm.

The train was ultimately bound for my uncle and aunt, Harold and Doreen in Surrey, and on my first morning there I heard of the death of Carl Jung on the radio. I took this as auspicious for I particularly liked the writings of the Swiss psychologist. My relations had told me that nearby Guildford Technical College had a reputation as one of the best crammers for university entrance in the south of England and so I went for interview.

I was seen by a Mr Hopkins, a big burly man with kind eyes behind small horn-rimmed glasses. In vain, he tried to persuade me to study technical subjects and take Maths and Physics, but I refused and instead signed up for A level English and History, as well as O level Latin and French. The next step to which I was not looking forward was my return visit home.

I arrived on a Saturday morning wearing my Italian style clothes and, as I walked the length of the beach path towards home, I felt good. Mother was there and welcomed me with open arms. Joss, now twelve, looked at me as if expecting to find something wrong. The three of us talked non-stop over an Ulster fry and cups of Nescafé and my mother told me that Father had found my letters from England so depressing that he had ultimately stopped opening them. After breakfast, I walked on the beach with Joss and we collected a few pieces of wood. Tears came to our eyes as we recalled his standing on the bungalow roof when I had left home four years earlier.

Father, now working as an animal trapper with the Forestry Commission, returned at lunchtime. He was not pleased to see me.

'So, you're back!' he remarked before going off to change out of his work clothes. Mother went off after him and I heard raised voices.

'I hope he doesn't think he's going to be staying here,' he said angrily but my mother reassured him that I was going to study in Guildford Tech and would be leaving soon.

On my last day at home, still smarting from Father's reaction, I stood on the shore and drank in my surroundings: it was a chilly day and the sea was choppy. I stayed there, mesmerized by the waves and the rattle of shingle.

A YEAR LATER I was ready for him; I had achieved the req-
uisite GCE exams for university entrance and had written
to tell my parents that I had been offered a place at Trinity
College, Dublin. When I arrived at the bungalow, Mother's
delight was apparent while Father said little but looked in
reasonable humour. It was not till later that he spoke and at
teatime he asked me what I was going to study; I replied that
I was going to do philosophy.

'Philosophy?!' he almost shouted, 'What in the name of
God do you want to study philosophy for?' He paused, went
back to eating and the only sound was of him chewing.

'Philosophy – of all things,' he muttered to himself and the
subject was not mentioned again that evening.

In the morning I told my mother I would take the midday
train to Dublin.

'Not at all – your Father's going to drive you,' she said.

I gaped at her in disbelief as Father suddenly appeared for
breakfast.

'Are you sure you want to drive all that way?' I said.

'Ah, I'll hardly be there till I'm back again,' he replied.
'Here, I'll give this to you now,' and reaching into his trouser
pocket handed me a warm roll of banknotes.

At eleven we climbed into his battered Vauxhall Victor
and Mother held the railway gate open as we drove over the
lines through Loughview farmyard and up the Orange Hall
lane. As we bumped along, hedges brushing the windows he
said he wanted to avoid the newly built M1 motorway as he
didn't like driving on it.

As we drove into Belfast, I realized that it wasn't just the
M1 that was bothering him – he was not a confident city
driver and we soon lost our way, to end up two hours later

somewhere in south County Down. Eventually we emerged on to the coastline near Annalong and as we made our way towards Carlingford Lough we gazed out at the vista of a wind-torn sea lit by blazing sun.

'Isn't this a lot better than a motorway, now?' he said and I had to agree.

We arrived in Dublin four hours late and when we joined heavy traffic passing the front of Trinity College he was too nervous to pull in, so we continued round into Nassau Street, where he set me down at the back gate of the college beside the porter's lodge.

'Thanks,' I said.

'Well, I'll not stay,' he replied. I stood and watched as, shakily, he moved off and, narrowly missing a street pigeon, rejoined the traffic.